WHEN I THINK ABOUT POWER

ERIC HART JR.

Everyday of my life I've been called my father. And while I've watched
my face mature into a replica of his, watched my beard fill in the same
way his sits, and grew to a height tall enough to see him eye to eye,
there are certain characteristics I could never seem to match. The
stride in his walk, the tone of his voice, but most importantly, the
pride in himself. The type of pride that exudes a certain confidence,
a certain power.

Growing up as a queer black man in Southern America, power
hid from me. Almost like a game of hide and seek. I searched and
searched. Followed the tracks of others. Tracks that led me to pews of
judgment, in between sheets of temporary satisfaction, and ultimately
to a place of always questioning who looked back at me in mirrors.
It wasn't until this search led me to photography that I began to
understand this person. Through photographic expression I have
begin to find my own tone of voice, my own stride, my own power.
This collection is an expression of my journey.

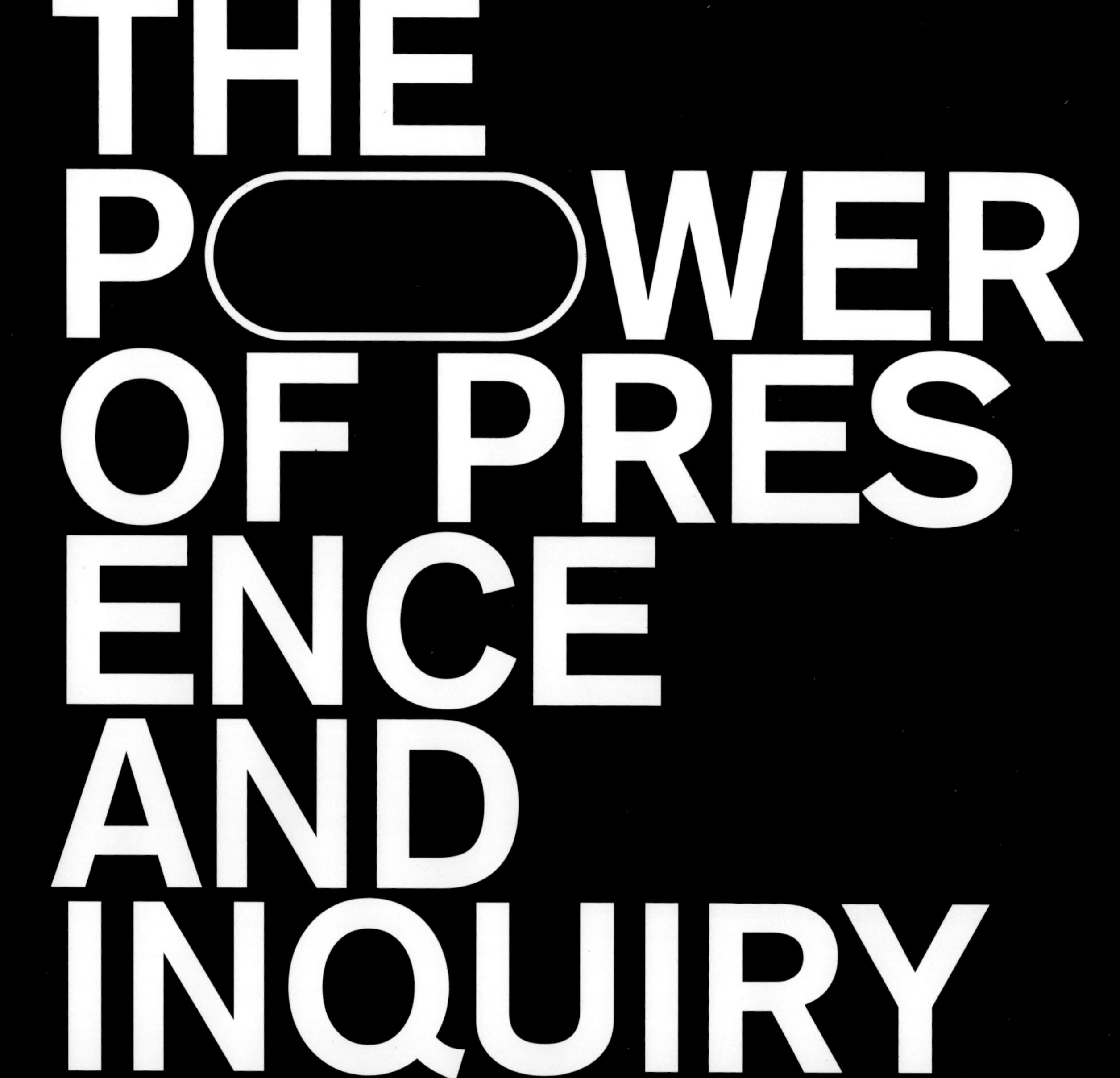
THE
POWER
OF PRES
ENCE
AND
INQUIRY

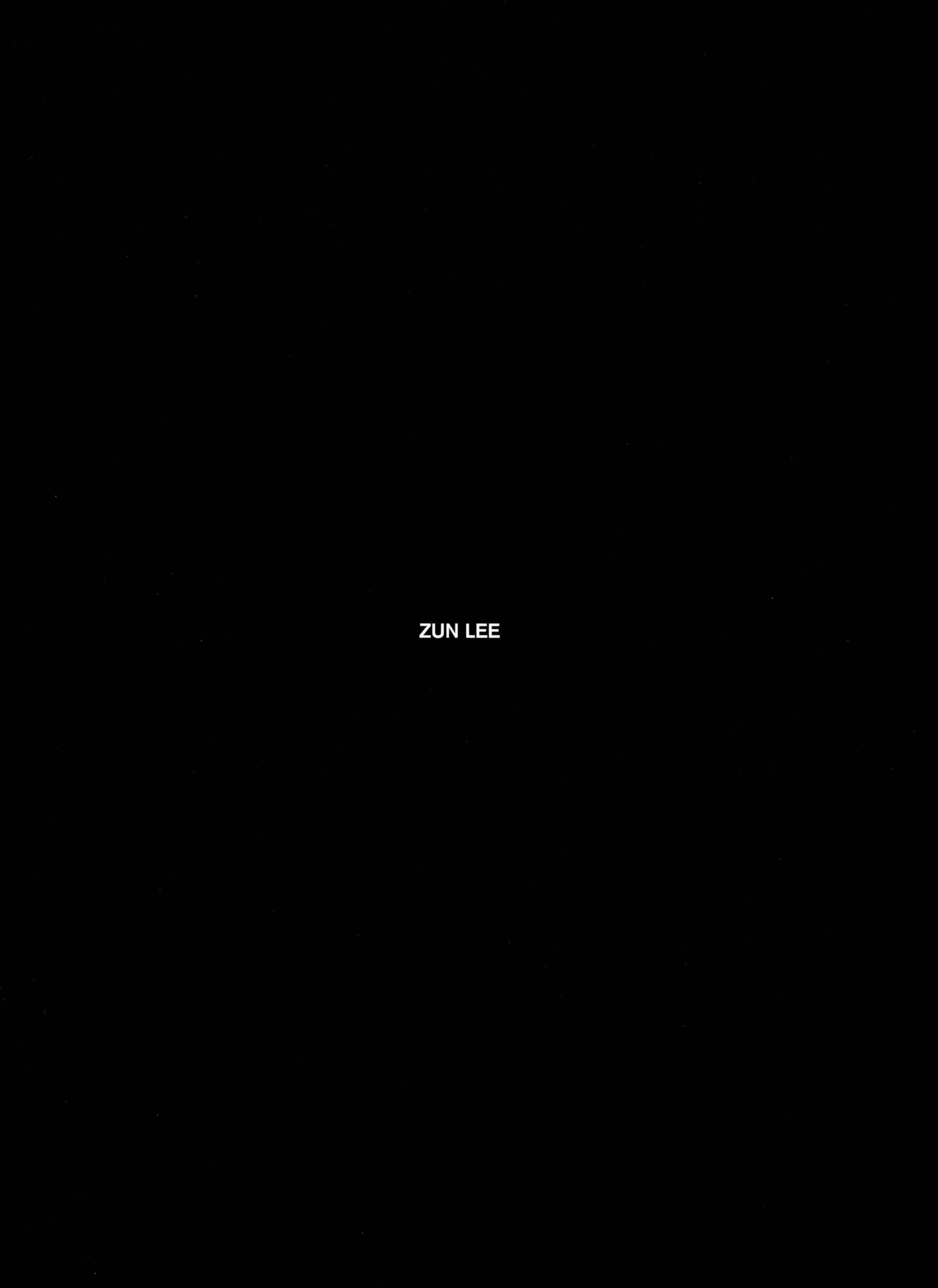
ZUN LEE

"I knew you wasn't soft" - Kevin to Little in *Moonlight* (2016).

Power is such a broad and totalizing concept - often used to ascribe the forcefulness of transformation and change but also invariably associated with domination, control, discipline and subjugation, a struggle between hardened fronts: One side takes, the other seeks to counter and to reclaim.

Yet on an everyday basis, power tends to devastate in insidious ways: A court ruling signed by a majority of judges. A prescription for the "morning after pill" that can no longer be filled. Being summoned to work as an "essential worker" during a pandemic without access to proper safeguards. An eminent domain notice. A county clerk refusing to issue a marriage license to a same-sex couple. None of this is particularly interesting from a visual storytelling perspective because it lacks the kind of confrontational binary dynamic we have come to rely on as the tension between "good and evil", "right and wrong", "stasis and transcendence", "resilience and trauma". But we live in a time that again reminds us who exerts power over others (and how), and that this space is likely to remain forever contested. Images alone don't have the power to effect change. Conversations about visibility and representation rarely explore the realm of personal agency in the presence of regulation. It remains easier to create a visual facsimile of what power may connote than to actually question these dynamics in real life.

So where can we locate the transformative possibilities of power? Can the idea of power be divested from its racial, cisheteropatriarchal logic? What would a re-queering of power mean and what would it look and feel like? Can the inquiry itself be foregrounded rather than relying on a notion of oppositional resistance that only reinforces the original oppressive logic? Enter the imaginative constellation of Eric Hart Jr.'s portraiture work. Right away, the minimal aesthetic and abundant negative space feel deeply introspective and open-ended, an invitation to a journey rather than a celebratory arrival. In an art world that privileges the fully-formed and declarative, it's rare to be granted access to a maker who is on a search and who lets us in on it. Make no mistake, Eric's combination of technical restraint and inquisitive depth is quite deliberate. Yet this work never feels finite - these portraits are both destinations and points of departure in ways that render the intersecting ideas of Blackness, queerness and masculinity unresolved. *When I Think About Power* makes room in our contemporary discourse for the not-yet-answered, not-yet-overdetermined: Maximum volume and color is often associated with a Black queer aesthetic. Eric instead insists on a quotidian performativity that demands attention but doesn't pulse with the steady 4/4 thump of a club tune. There's a precision to his chronicling, a core to his inquiry that reciprocates or even challenges our gaze but is never in-your-face and allows codes to hide in plain sight.

Eric examines Black queer power not only as a perfomative response to gender and patriarchal norms. His work problematizes the idea of how much of this normativity is already internalized and either becomes the source of internal conflict or is expressed in ways that reinforce rather than disrupt these intersecting norms. It reminds us that the idea of power is not only reified in control over others but over the self, pointing to a still-ongoing struggle to compensate for the refusal of personhood during slavery, when it was impossible for Black men to own or control anything, including their selfhood. No wonder that normative masculinity too often remains predicated on this idea of self-control or restraint: *Don't show emotion. Boys don't cry. Don't be a sissy. Don't be loud.*

Eric isn't content with simple acts of reclamation or tableaus that offer legible visions of an "end game". He also refrains from judgment about what is "good" or "bad", "complete" or "incomplete". He offers a more pared-down yet wide-open body of work that not only incorporates many different lines of inquiry but forces us to ask questions of ourselves.

This is especially helpful given a contemporary visual culture where mainstream discourse tends to expropriate from the margins a certain kind of Black queerness, a certain kind of Black queer masculinity, as the desirable aesthetic. Often, this aesthetic augurs a queer futurity of fully-actualized freedom but Eric focuses on a more down-to-earth kind of practice of questioning. The two aren't mutually exclusive. One can luxuriate in the grand, magical, extravagant, and joyful displays of Black queerness so eagerly desired and consumed globally as ways to emancipate and liberate oneself. Or, we can appreciate that the idea of Black queer power contains many alternate practices of freedom that each require courage and work here and now, not just transcendent heterotopias.

Maybe that begins with how we deliberately acknowledge our presence with one another. Eric's personal desire to not only be seen but to have his authentic presence affirmed - by friends, by lovers, by his own kinfolk - that desire unfolds in the way he sits with his collaborators and what his collaborators mirror back to us. There is a generosity that shouldn't feel so refreshing in its straightforwardness and honesty. Yet in this overwrought culture of virtuous visibility that mistakes "oblique" for "opaque", privileges representation over actual practice, and that is still coming to terms with the insidious staying power of cisheteropatriarchal white supremacy, this work matters even more.

In a 1961 interview, James Baldwin remarked: "All you are ever told in this country about being Black is that it is a terrible, terrible thing to be. Now, in order to survive this, you have to really dig down into yourself and recreate yourself, really, according to no image which yet exists in America. You have to impose, in fact - this may sound very strange - you have to decide who you are, and force the world to deal with you, not with its idea of you." You have to decide - that work is not a process that tends to culminate in glorious discovery. It is rather a tedium of constant renegotiation, a balancing act between a set of imperfect choices and immovable constraints. And to examine what it means to show up and be seen in this struggle, this specific idea of presence, is neither inconsequential nor reductive: It is a reminder that America continues to oppress on a much more fundamental level: They don't (only) negate you because you're effeminate, flamboyant, shrill, colorful or sassy. They negate you simply because you exist.

Here, the idea of power becomes a pragmatic one. Rather than looking at unattainable aspirations of an uncertain future, this work creates a still-underappreciated space to see the practice of questioning not as stunted imagination but a way to engage in an honest, personal discourse: What is working for me and what isn't? What is within my power to change and what (yet) isn't? This is particularly important in our present moment, in which the forces that erase us approach their annihilating calculus from an equally pragmatic angle.

Sit with these ideas long enough, and we may be able to decouple the idea of power from a gendered perspective of masculine (and strong) versus feminine (and weak). We can also acknowledge that we remain beholden by these very perspectives on a daily basis. It honors the fact that many of us continue to struggle with not-yet-undone internalized ways of knowing but at the same time are afforded an opportunity to move beyond atavistic paradigms. The Black male bodies locking eyes with us here are our kin, our friends, our lovers, they're us. We ought to show up with them in the same way they do. With a presence that generates connection and doesn't separate us by shaming, labeling or exceptionalizing.

Power lies in expressing our freedom to destabilize and to dream, create, question and explore. Am I my ancestors' wildest dreams? Perhaps. But we can be even more capacious: I can be my own wildest dreams, with a limitless future. Everything is possible but it all starts with the courage to be here.

When I was initially asked to write a short essay for this collection, I was immediately humbled by the opportunity to participate in something of such impact in the cultural arena. By the moment of this work's publication, I will have served in government as an elected official for over a year, most of it spent as the Chair of the New York City Council Committee on Cultural Affairs. While my duties have included oversight and discretion of billions of dollars that fuel and empower this special sector of the world's uncontested cultural capital, I cherish each opportunity to make my own contributions. To share thoughts on the meaning and experience Black, queer masculinity – or perhaps queer masculine Blackness or Black masculine queerness[1] – alongside photography of such gravity, is a privilege. These pages and the work contained are a gift to whoever holds them; I am honored to put words to their visual majesty.

Masculinity might be our oldest social construct, alongside its feminine counterpart. While we can't hope to trace its origins and path with any specificity, we understand it to be deeply interwoven with expectations of strength and power across much of the globe. This expectation fueled the Patriarchy – both the literal rulership of male kings and the social power held by men in society and family. Traditionally, a man is both expected and perceived to be strong.

Race, on the other hand, is a much newer social construct, designed with sinister intentionality to strip the humanity from the people of one continent to fuel the insatiable conquest of another. Ethnic identity had existed for thousands of years prior; the first-ever race was Black.

As the centuries progressed in the United States, the myths of Blackness were developed to perpetuate oppression through hatred and fear. Through speeches from politicians and propaganda in the media, we were declared a violent enemy.

Queerness stands apart, though. It's a reality as old as our species – with an identity to match – whose perception has been as fluid as its definition for millenia. Contrasting its general acceptance in Ancient Athens with widespread consignment to the "closet" in our living memories shows our path is anything but linear.

But that non-linear path led to this country, where an old guard clinging to power invested ever more time and energy into designating and denigrating a lower class if only to have something they could be above. The cruelty designed for a Black population was magnified when its targets were queer. As our oppression overlapped, our identity formed.

The Black queer man in the United States wears this history and lives its contradictions. As a man, he is expected to demonstrate strength. Being Black, his strength is a threat. To some, his queerness is passionate and loving. To others, vulnerable and meek. But the vulnerability of queerness makes him no less threatening, his Black masculinity unshakable.

Viewed with suspicious eyes and restrained by violent arms, we turned inward to our own community for sanctuary and for fulfillment.

Today we live in an era of empowerment. While the agents of oppression are not gone, we have the power of self-definition and therefore the strength to resist; we will overcome them. This is not the raw, brute strength assigned to masculinity, but an elemental one radiating from love and community.

I ran for office expecting these overlapping identities to be an obstacle. In some ways, of course they were. But I found over the course of the campaign and my subsequent service in government that our role and status were changing, because we were changing them. I won the seat not despite who I am but because of it.

It is our community, forged in fire, that makes our identities assets rather than liabilities. At the intersection of some of the nation's oldest and deepest oppressions, we survive and therefore thrive.

For too long the Black man's invented strength has been villainized, his real strength feared. The queer man has been pushed aside. Work like that of this collection is so necessary because it is both a brave act of self-expression and of collectivism. Right alongside each brick thrown at Stonewall and each arm linked on Edmund Pettus Bridge, this art and labor of love is foundational to the source of our community's pride and power: solidarity.

---

1 This is a question with which we with intersectional identities often wrestle without even knowing: To say I am a Black queer man implies I am a queer man (identity) who is Black (adjective). To say I am a queer Black man is the inverse, a Black man (identity) who can be described as queer (adjective). Our choice of word order implies a ranking of affinities, even if unintentionally so.

IT'S GIVING SOLIDARITY

CHI OSSÉ

"PRECISELY AT THE POINT WHEN YOU BEGIN TO
DEVELOP A CONSCIENCE, YOU MUST FIND
YOURSELF AT WAR WITH YOUR SOCIETY."

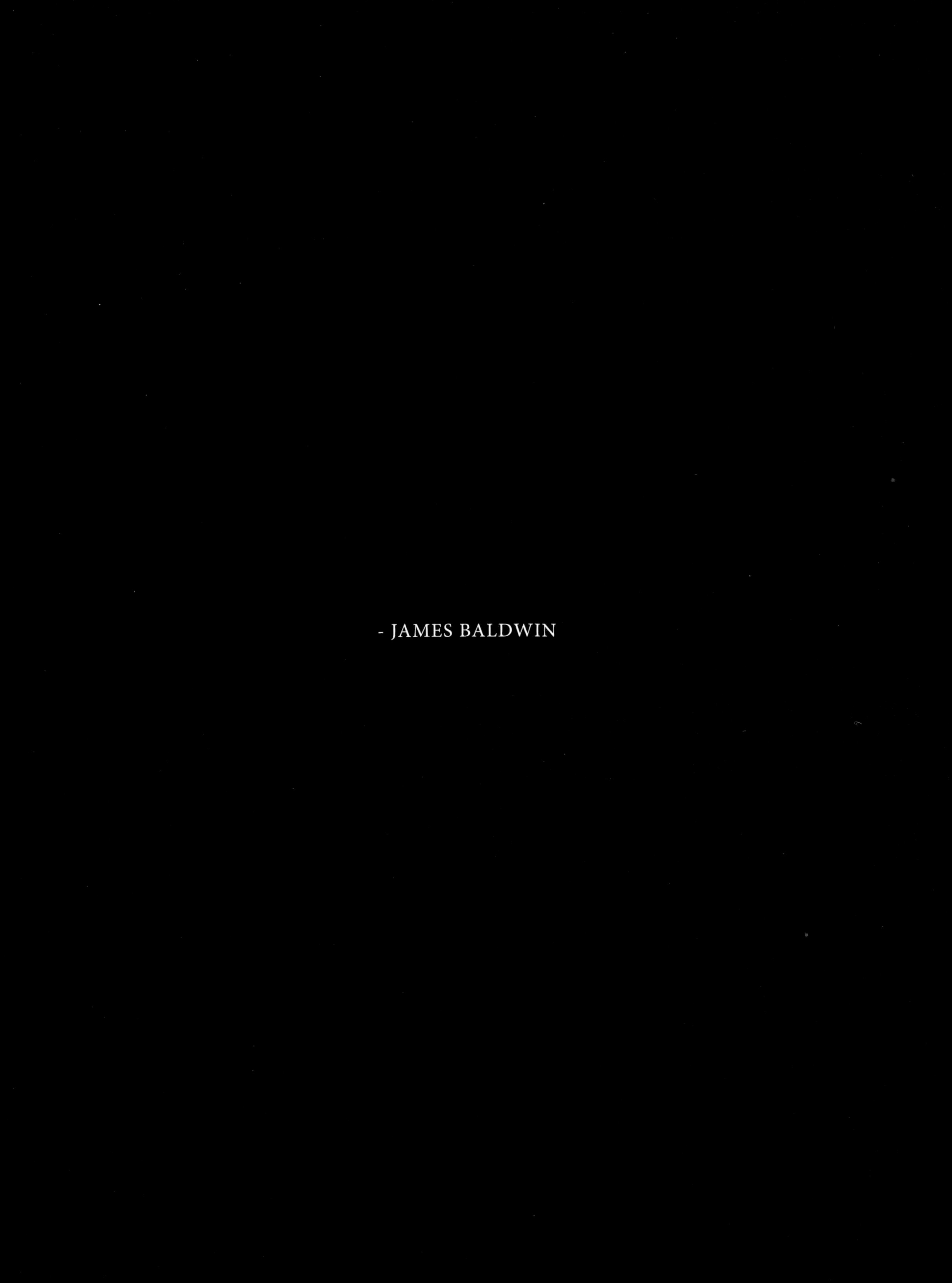

- JAMES BALDWIN

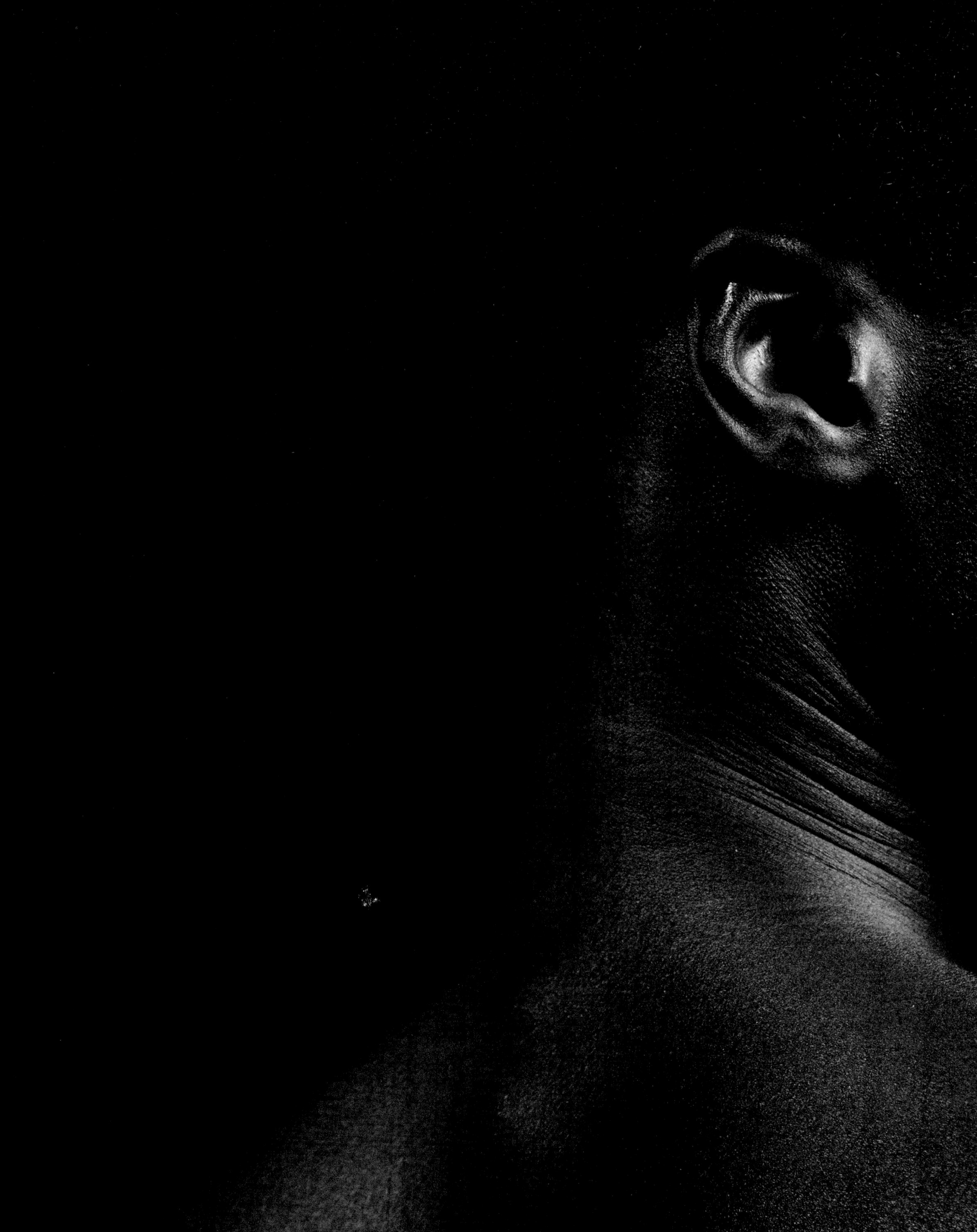

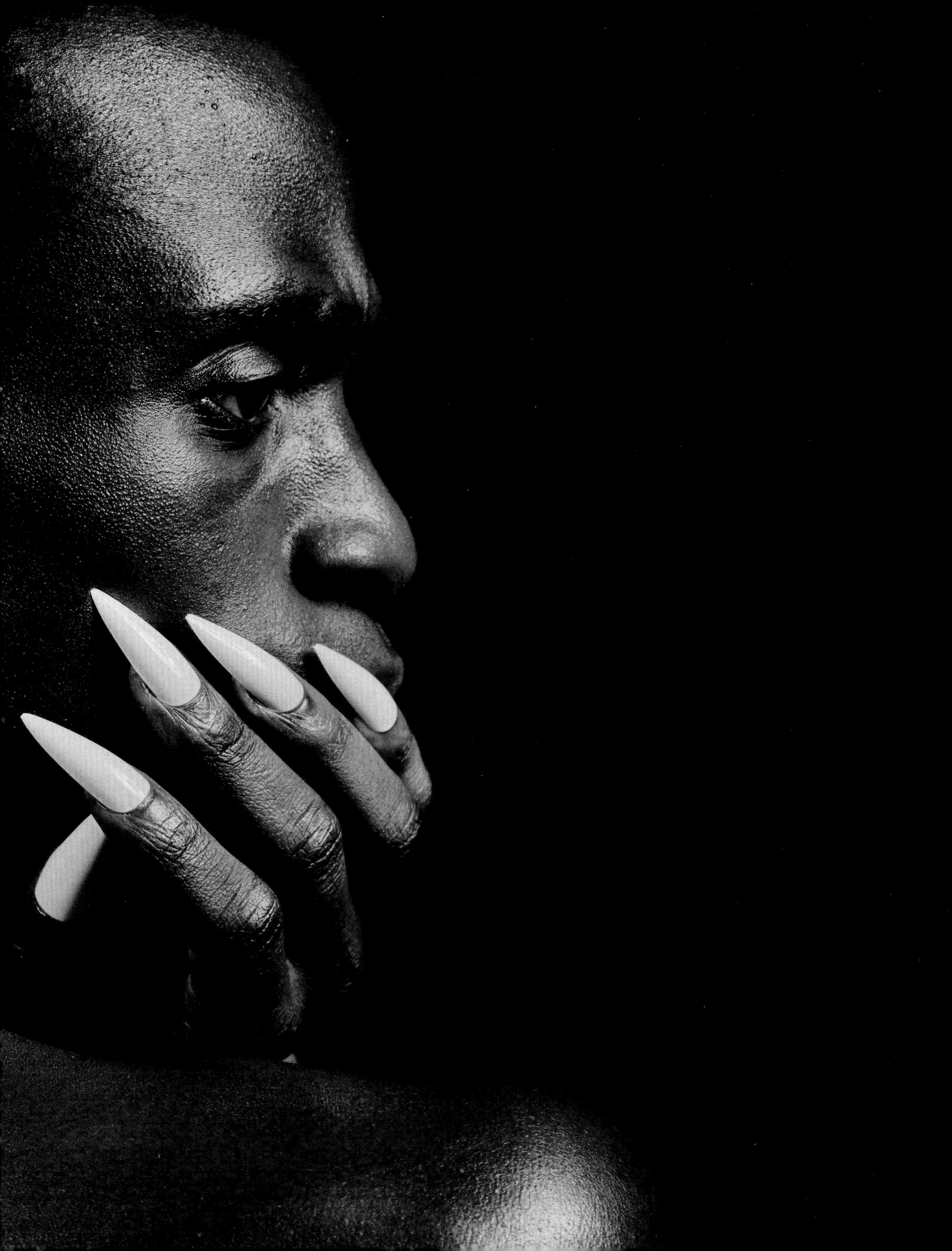

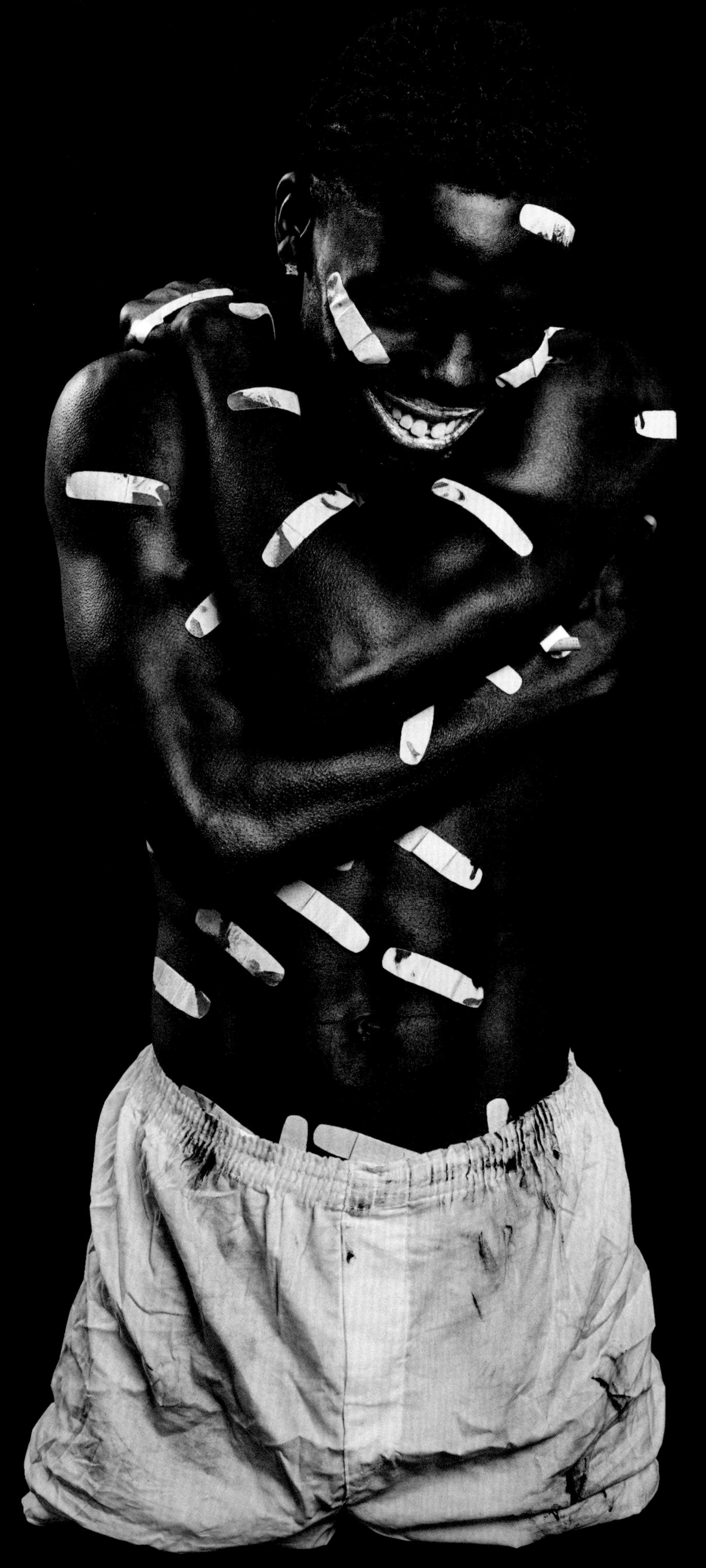

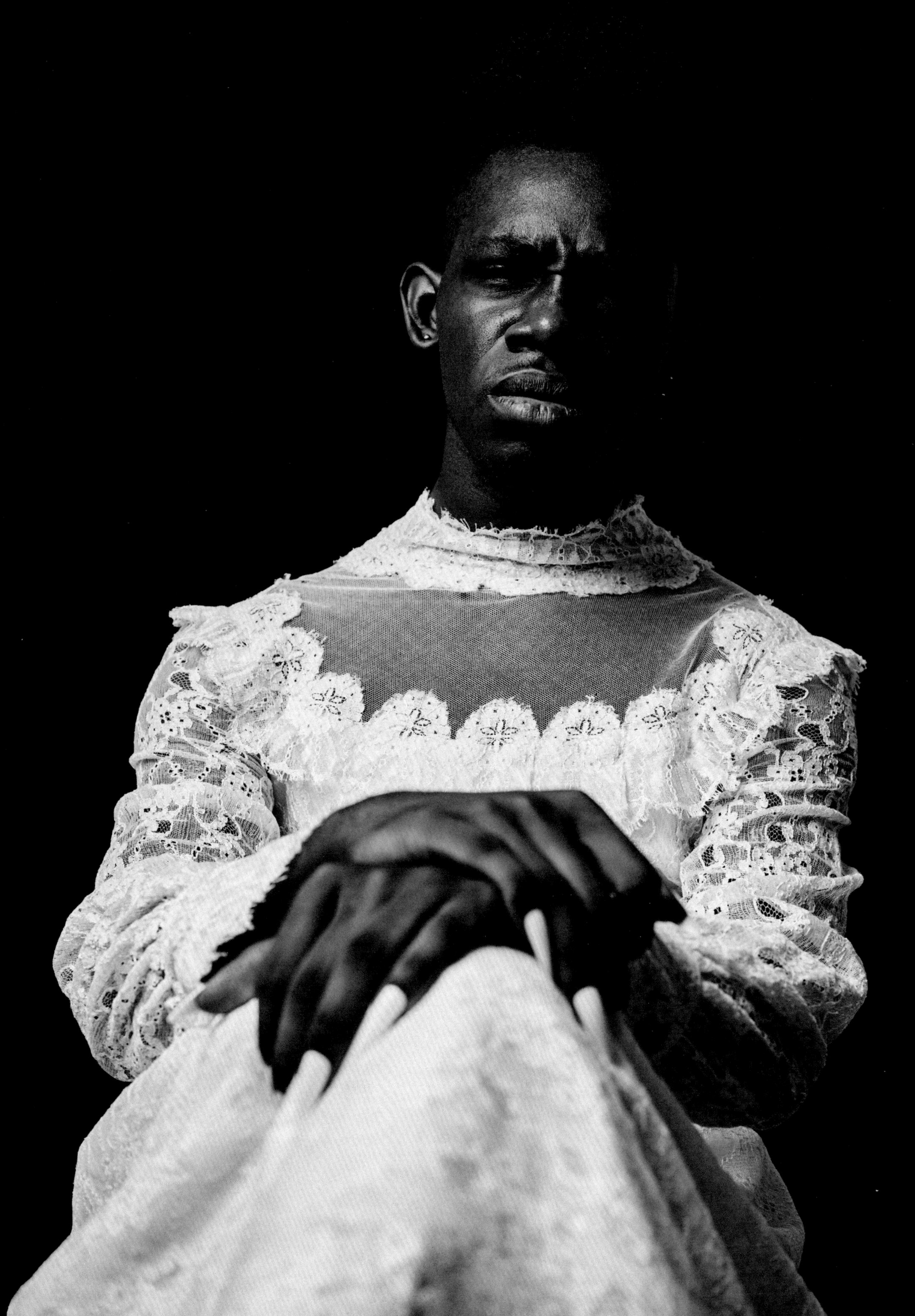

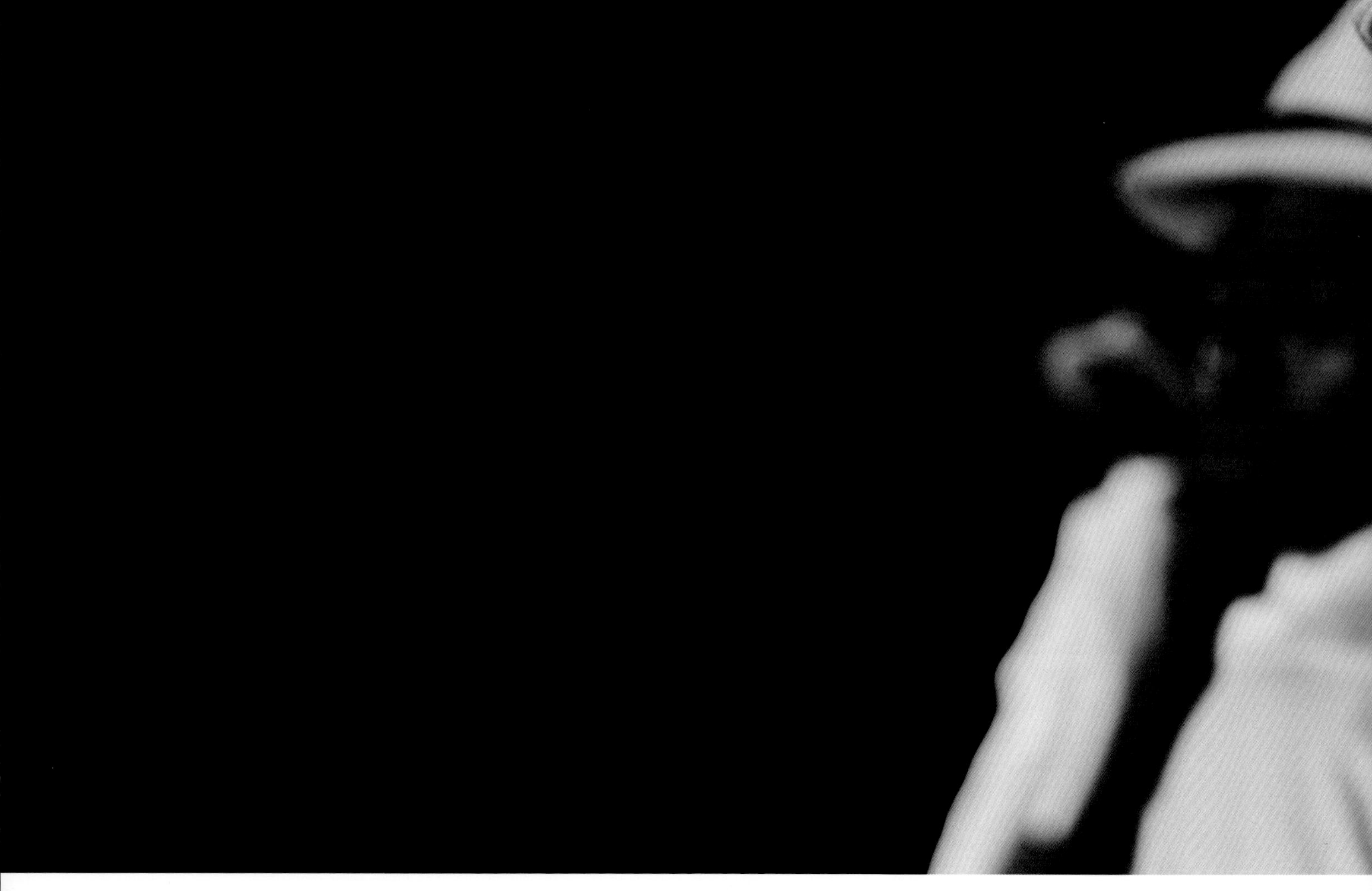

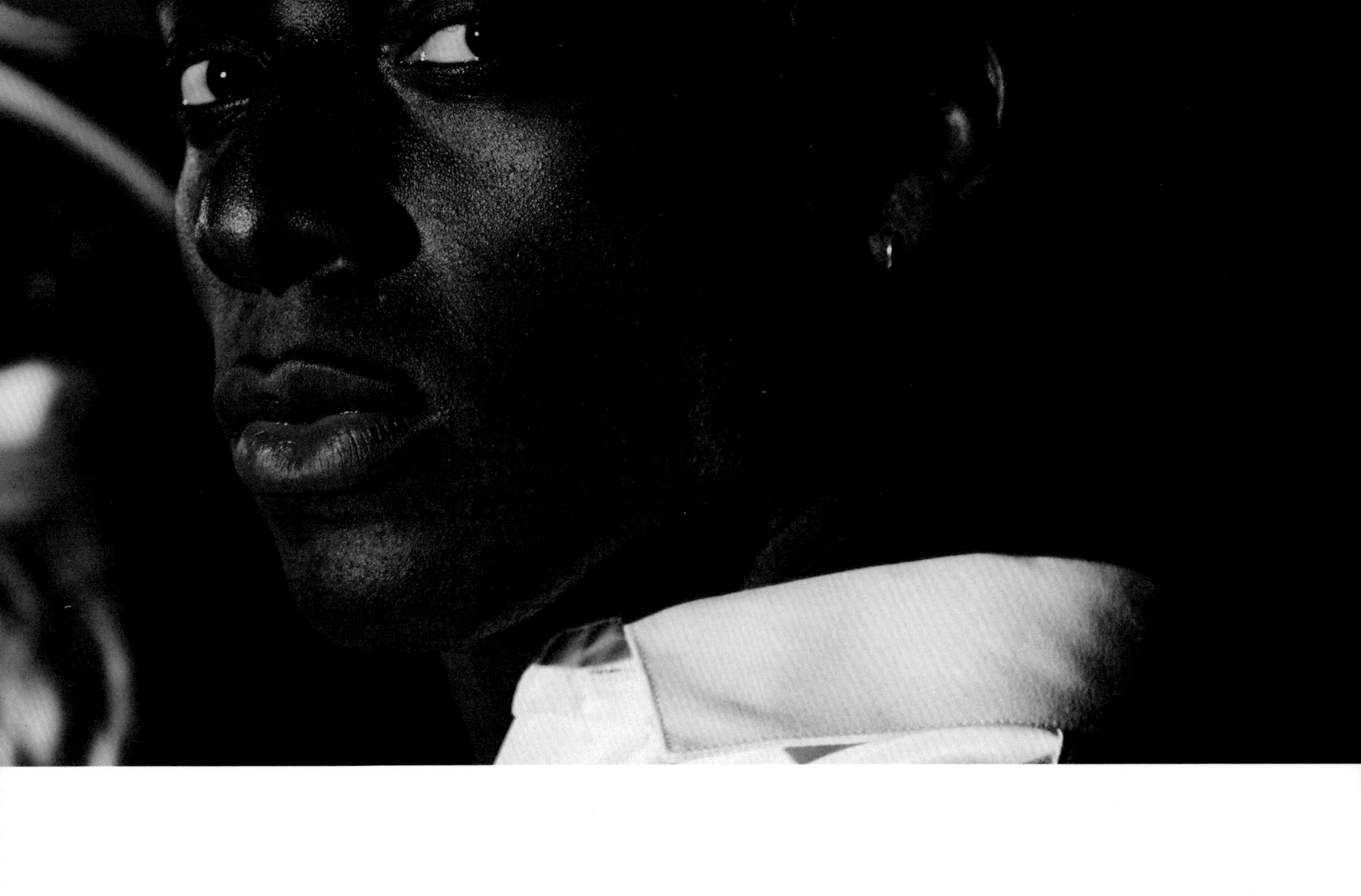

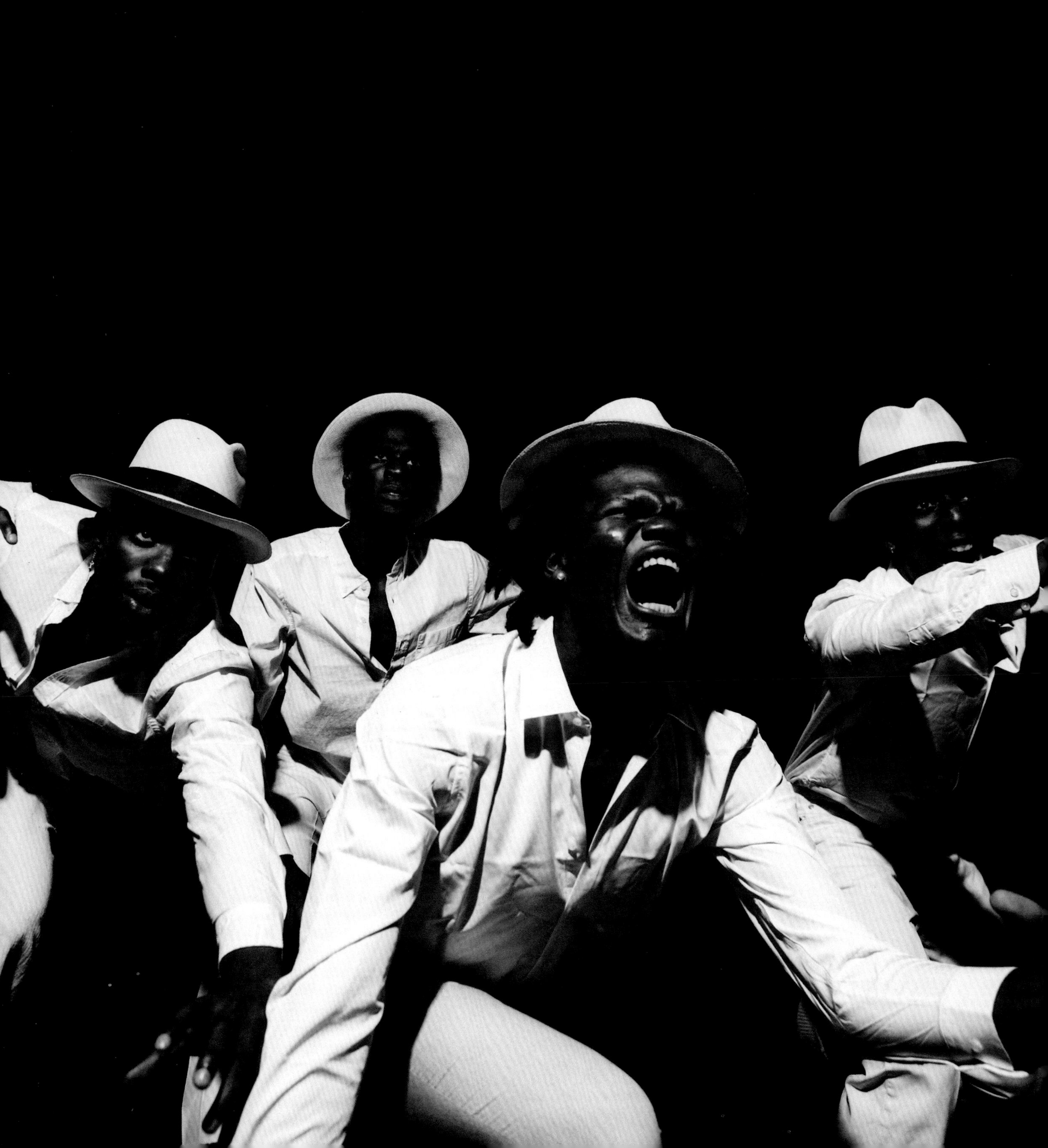

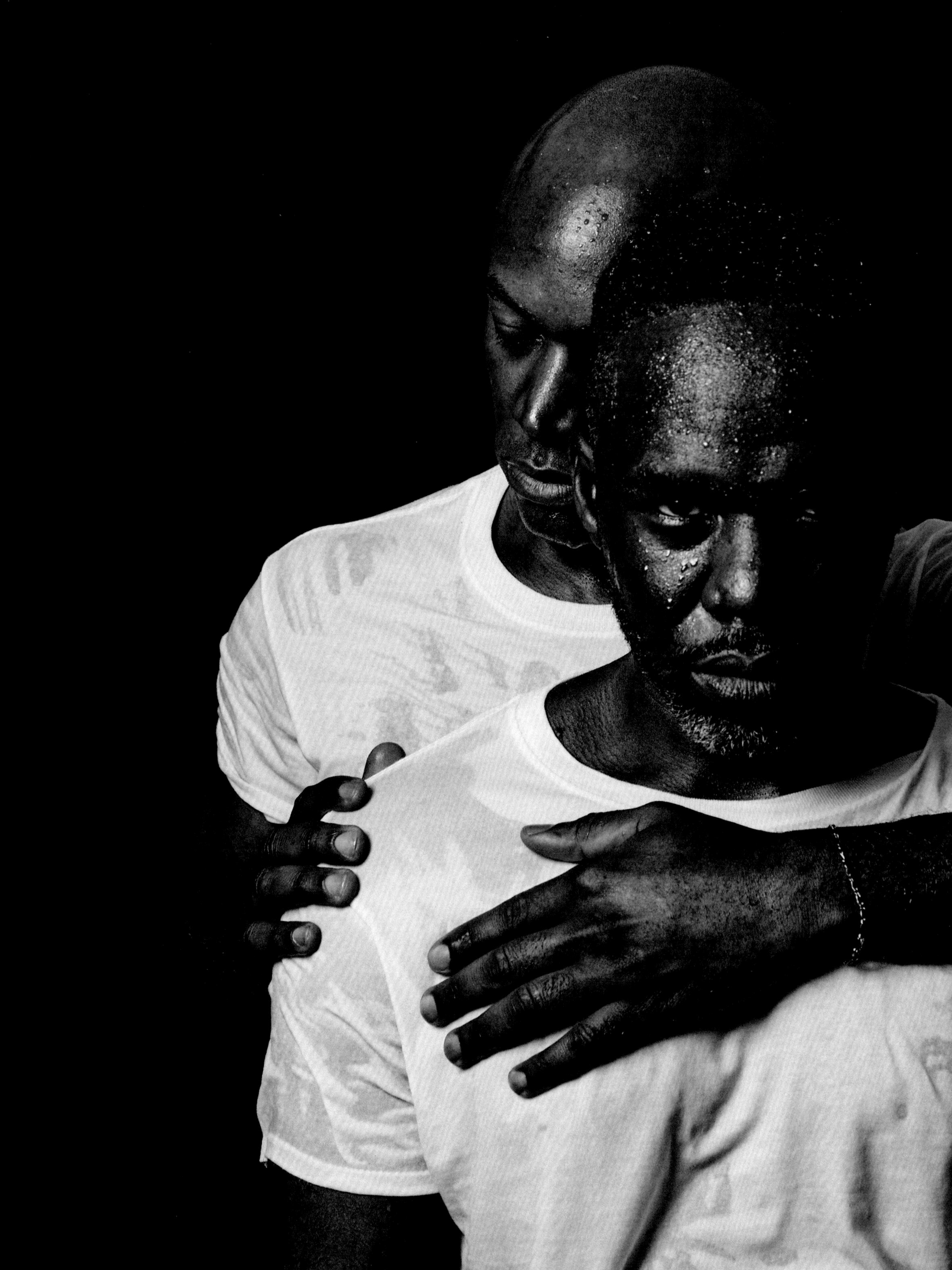

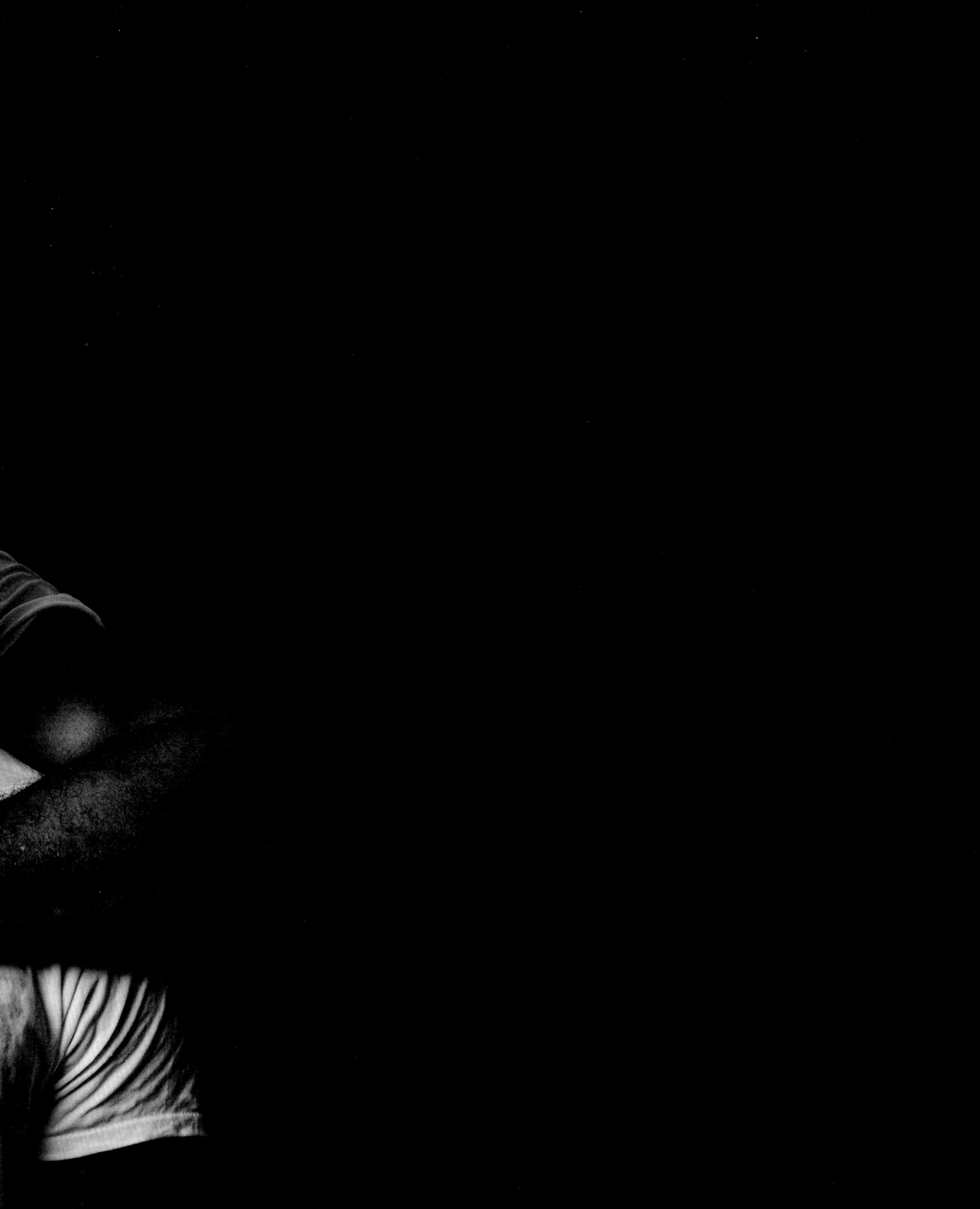

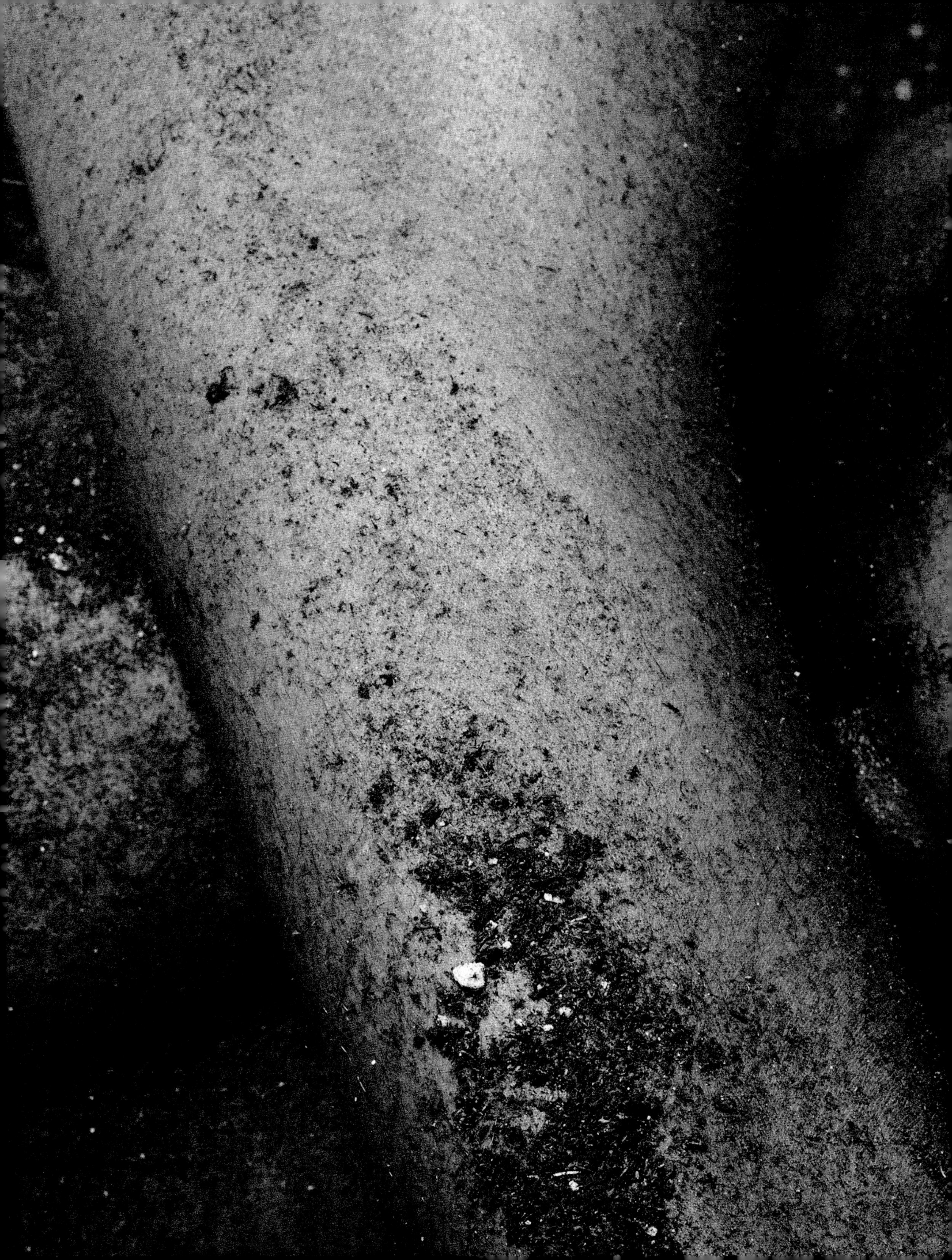

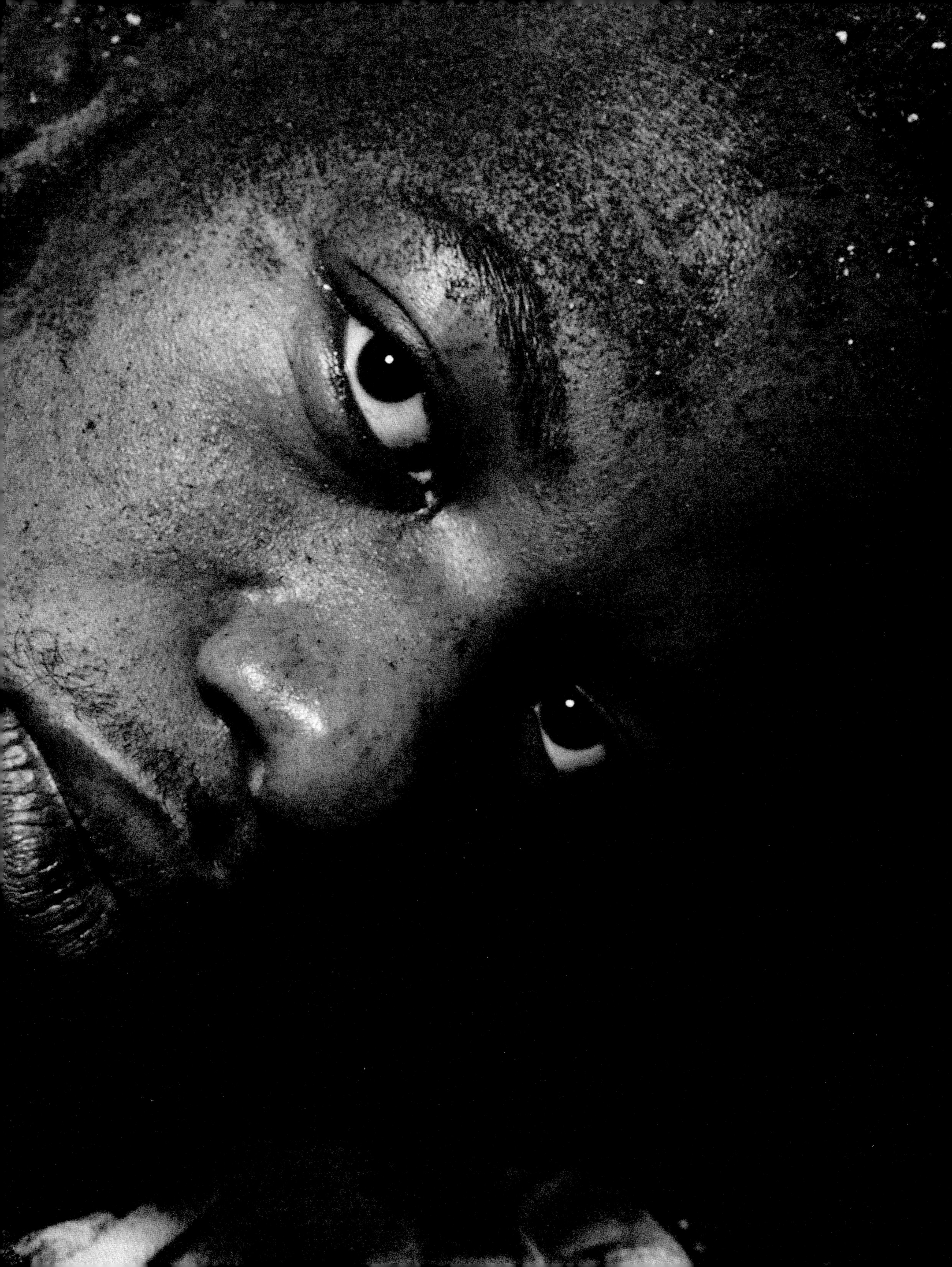

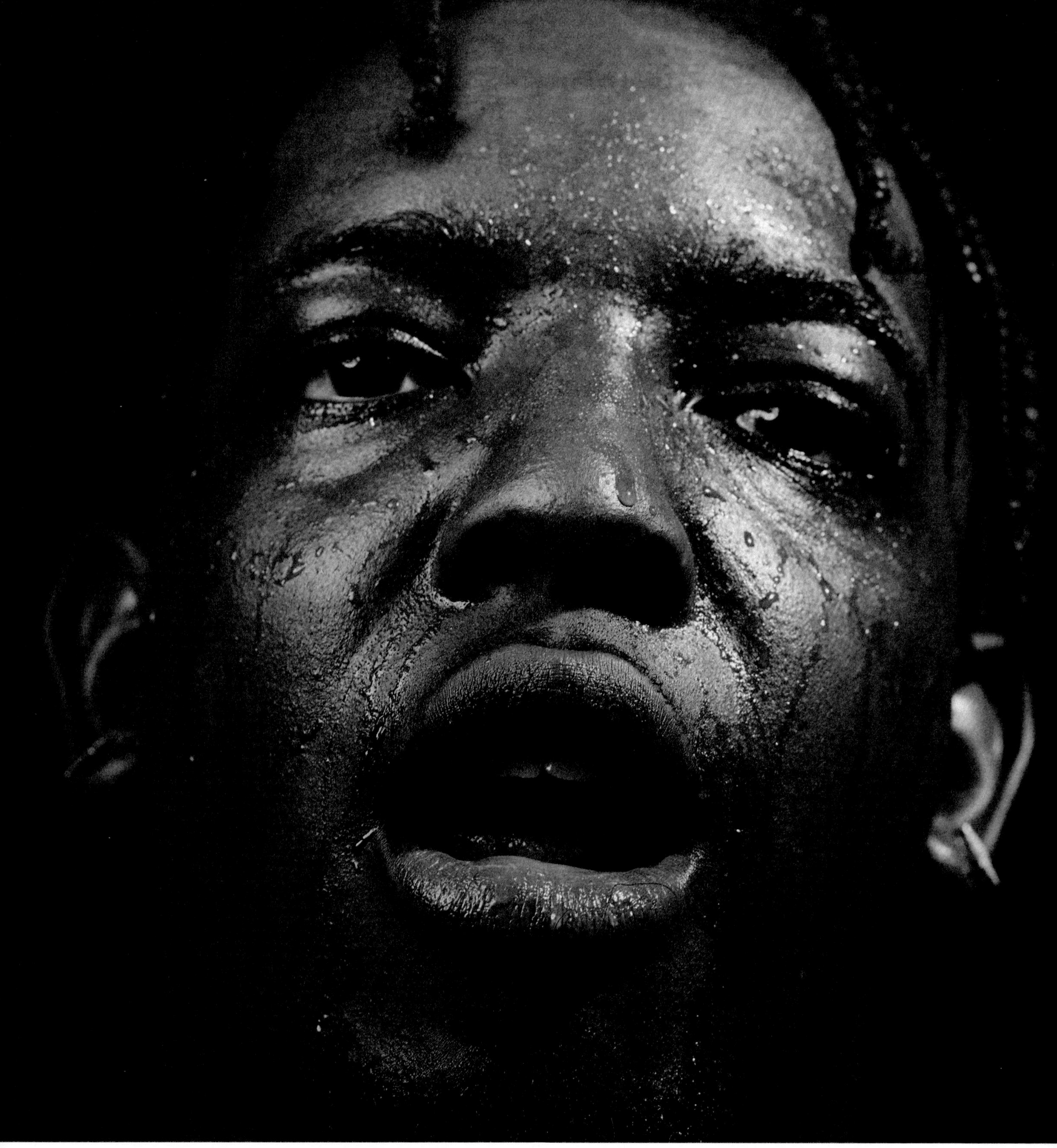

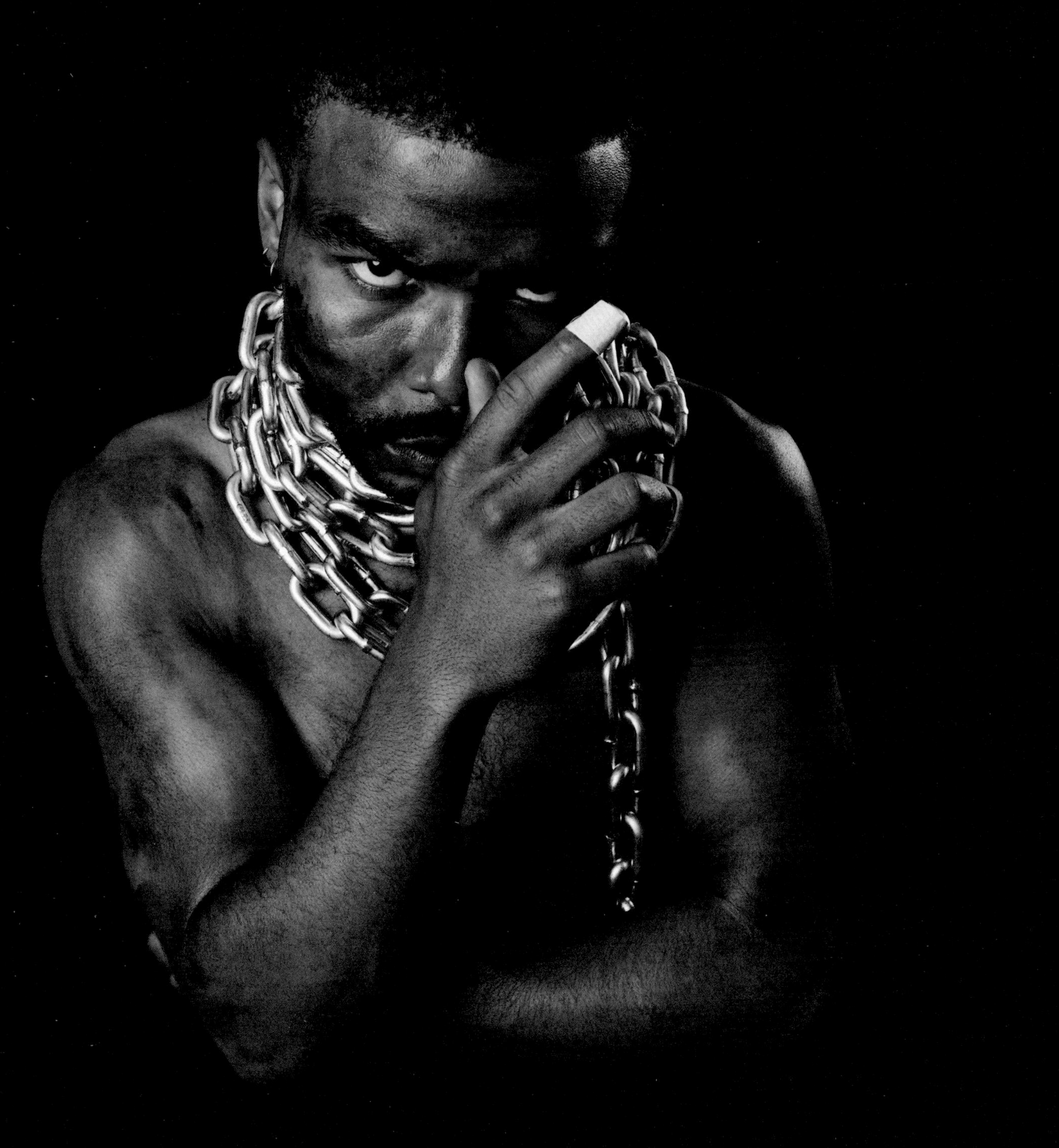

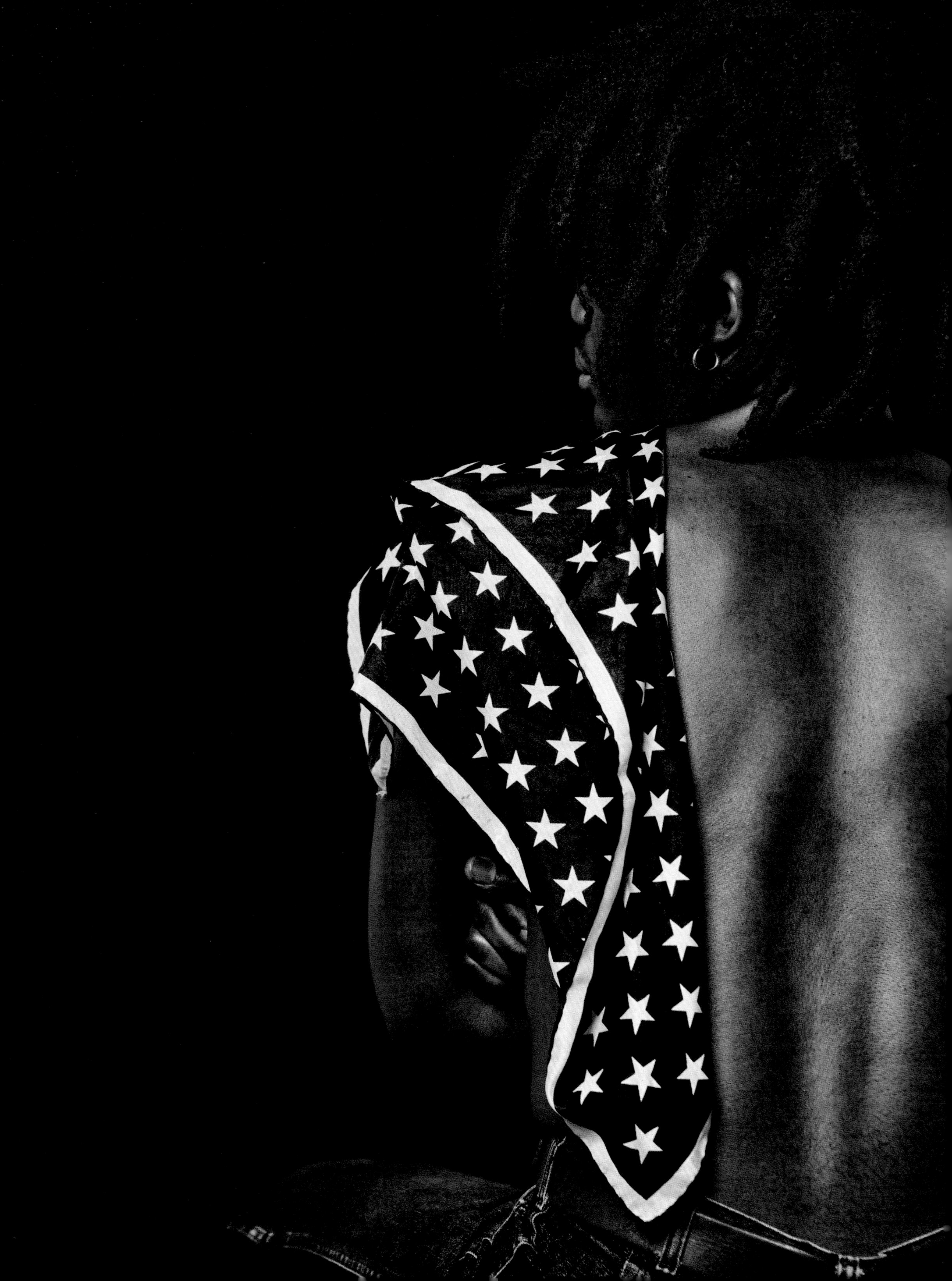

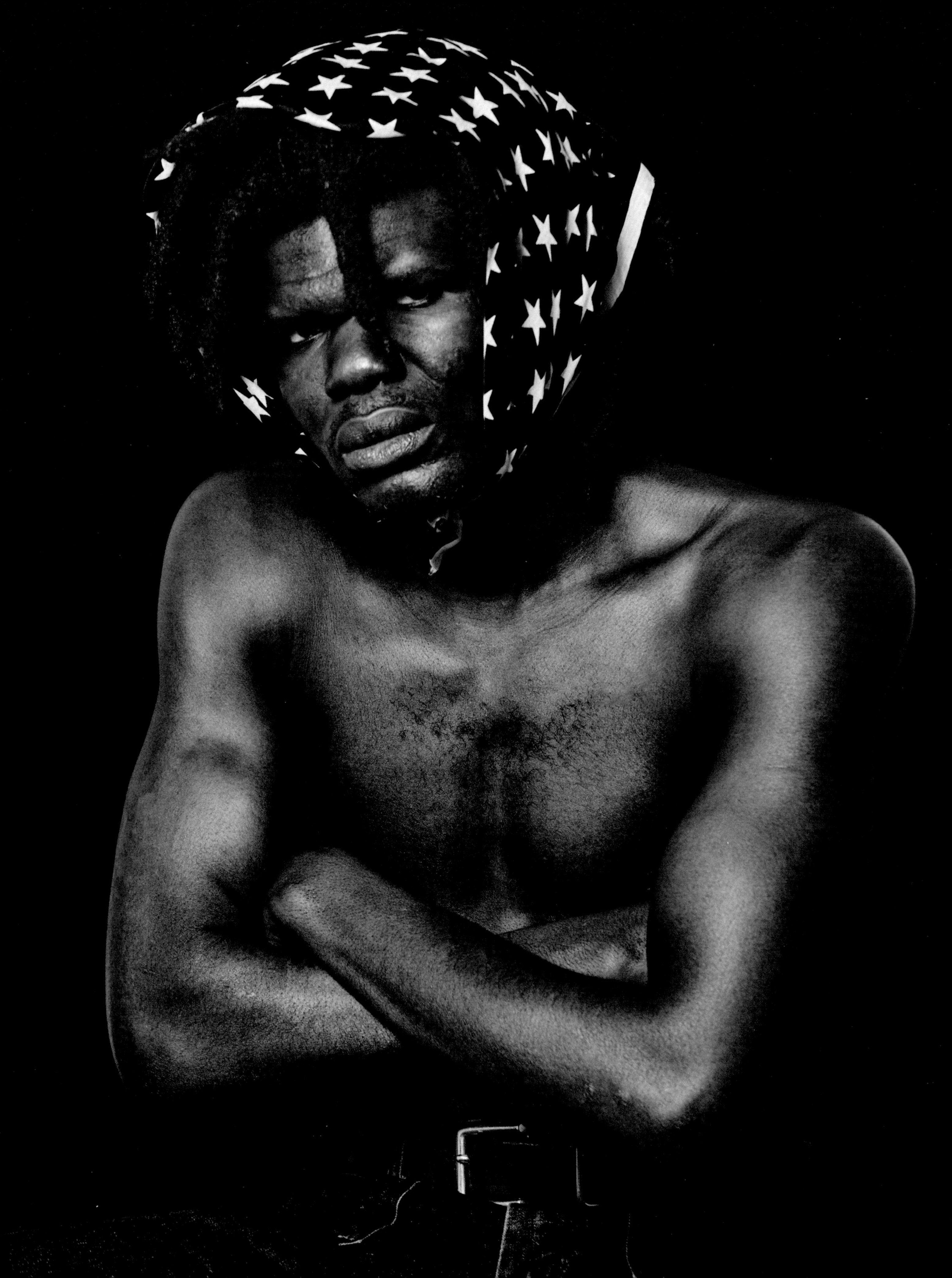

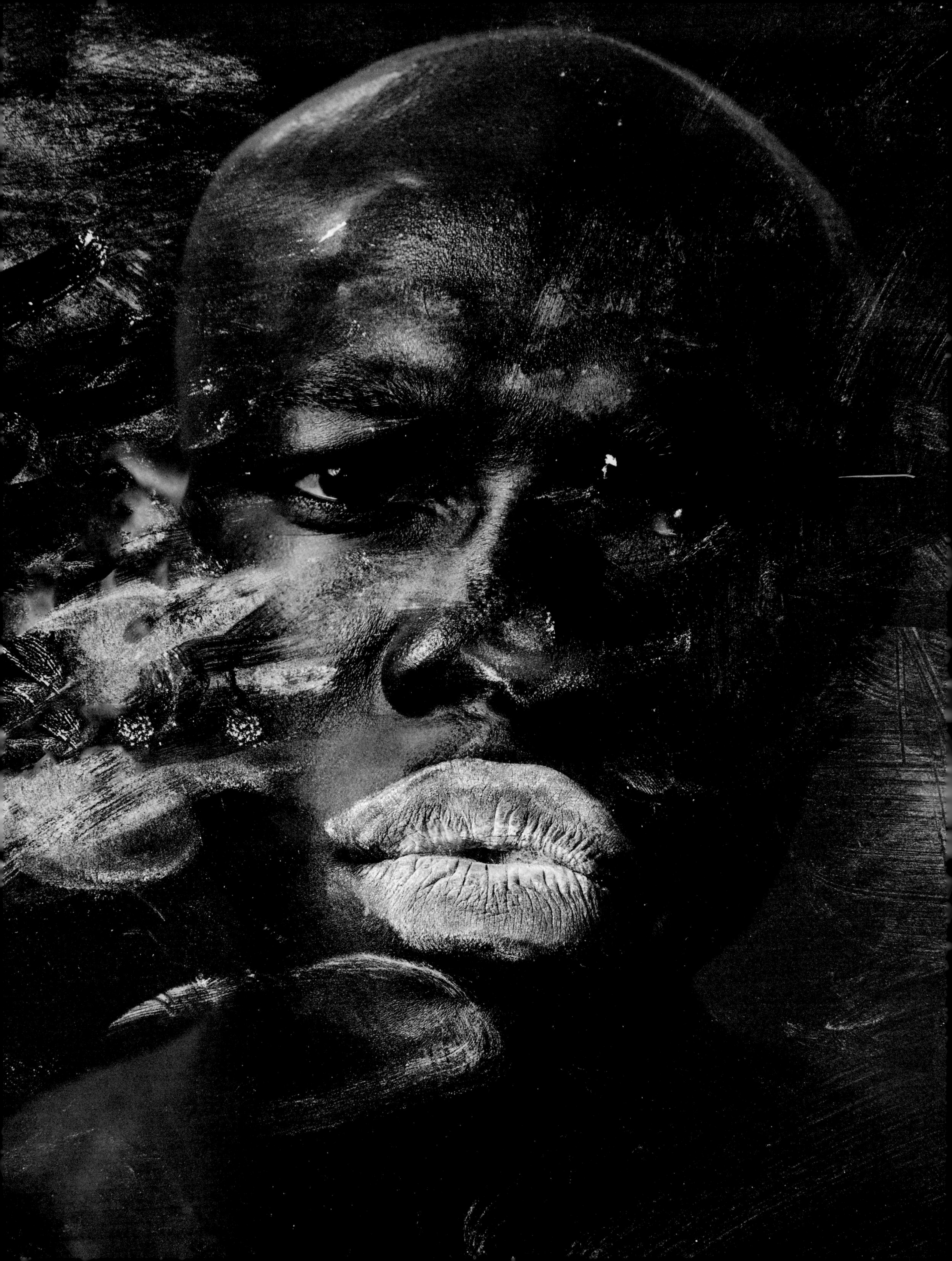

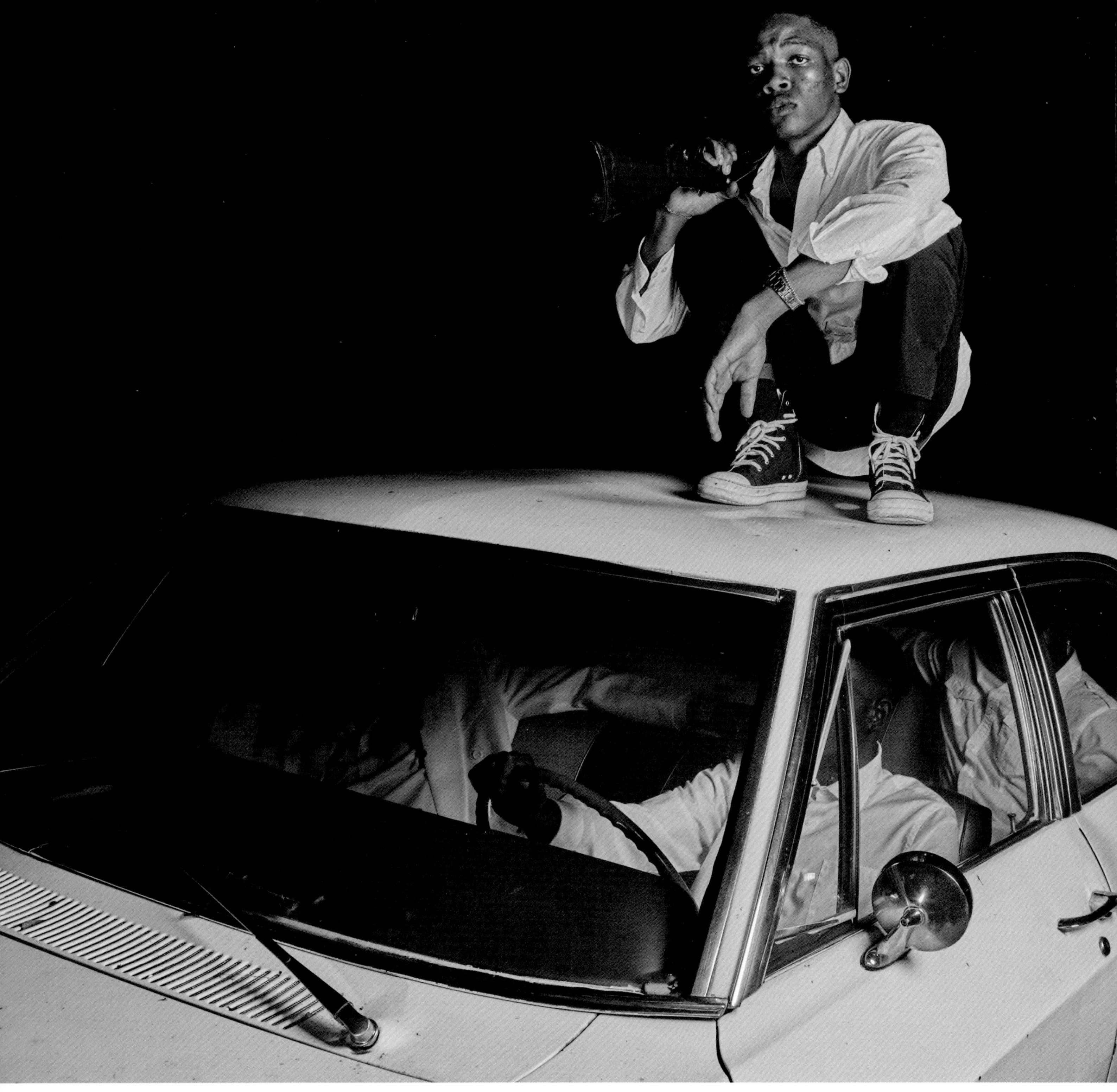

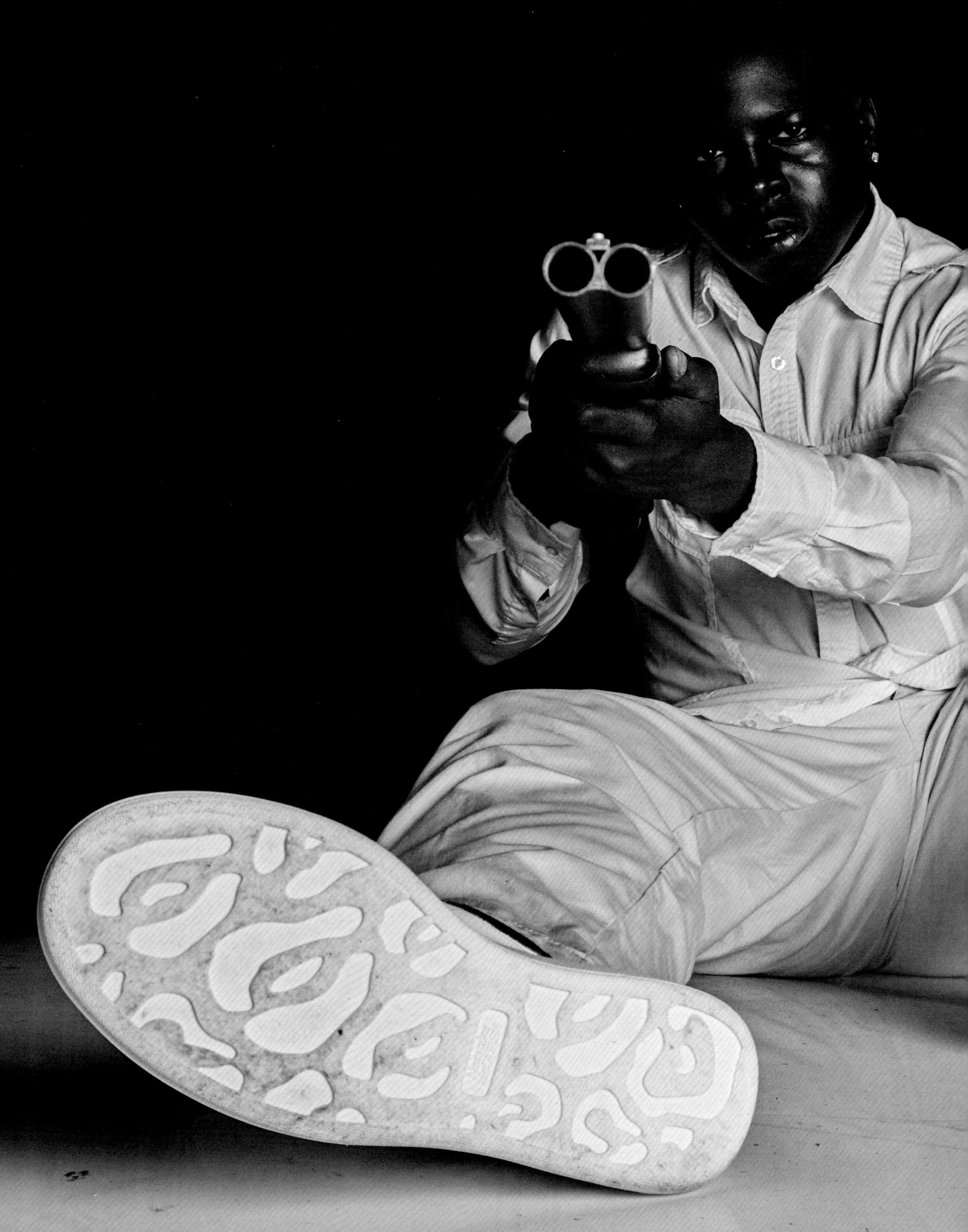

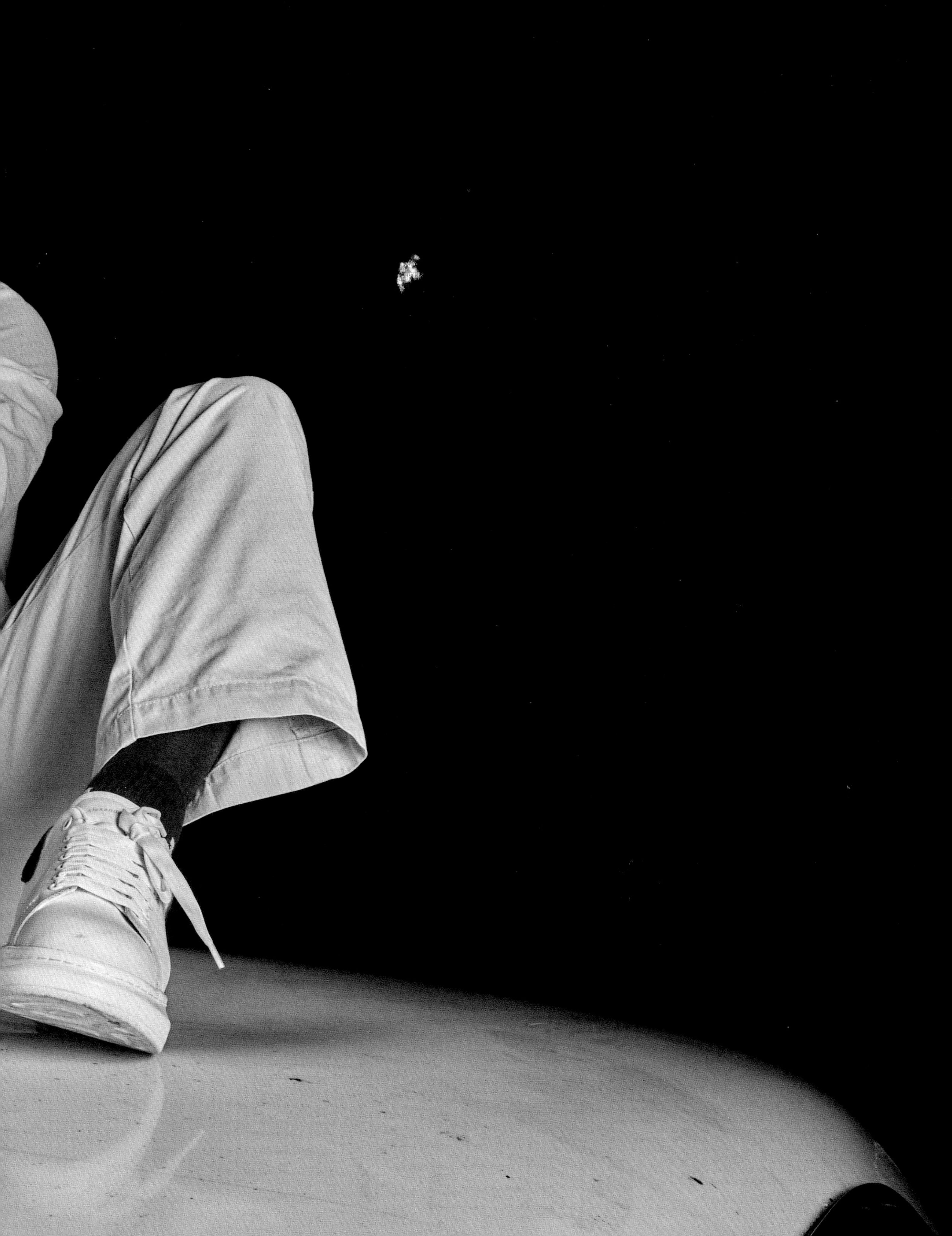

"SO MUCH OF MY LIFE HAS BEEN ABOUT
SELF-EFFACEMENT, PRETENSE, MASQUERADING,
CONCEALMENT, AND INDIRECTION"

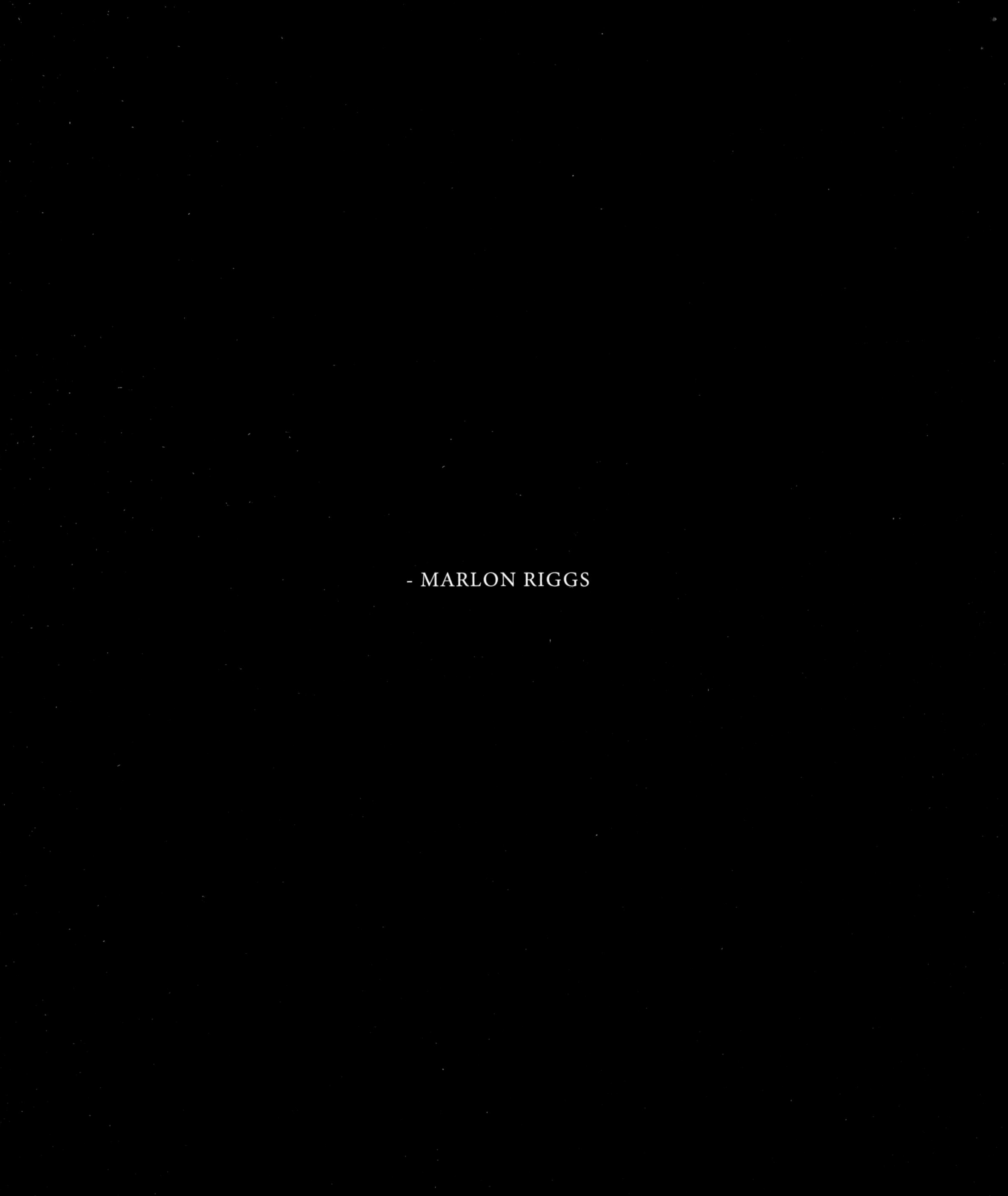
- MARLON RIGGS

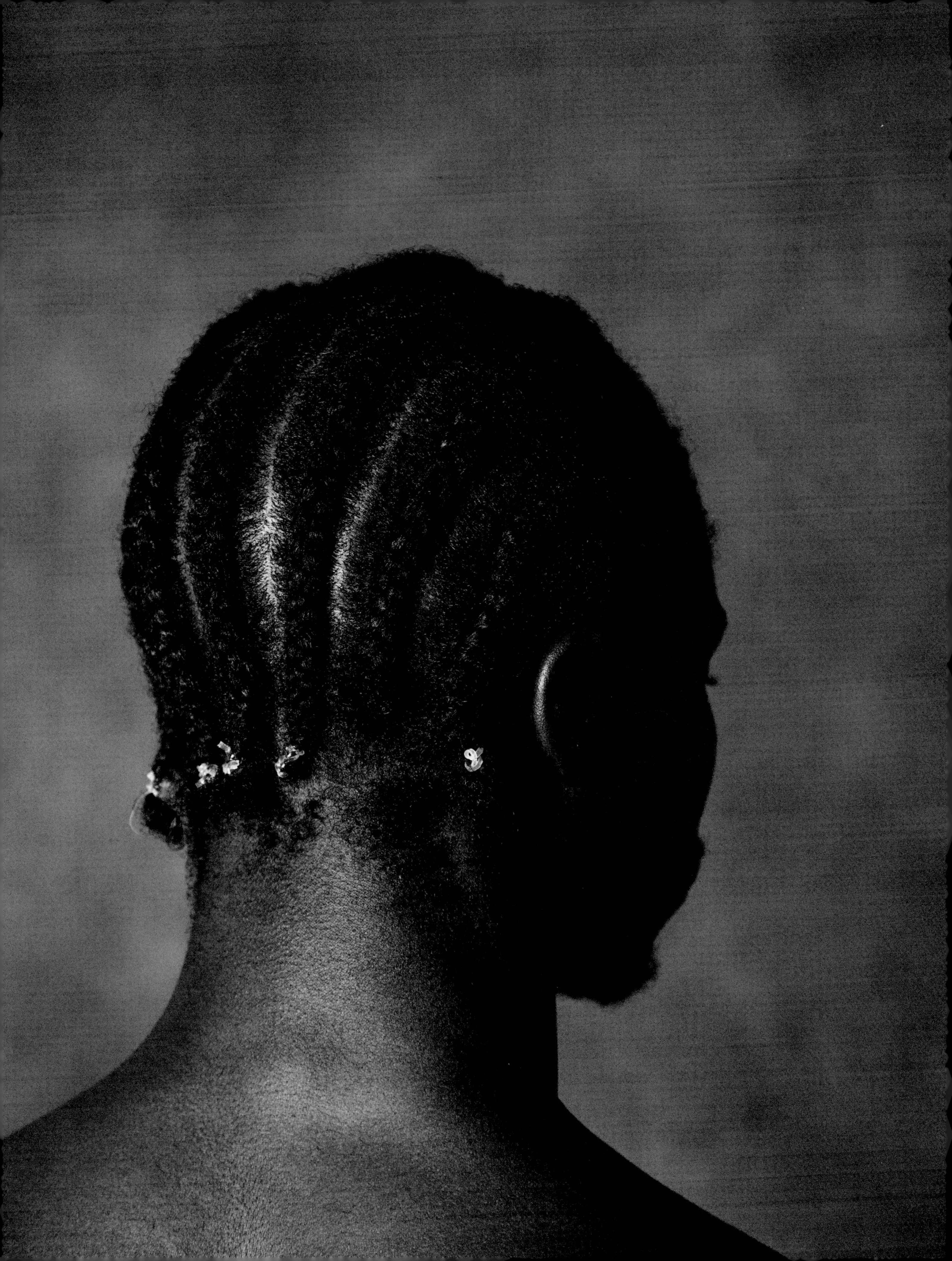

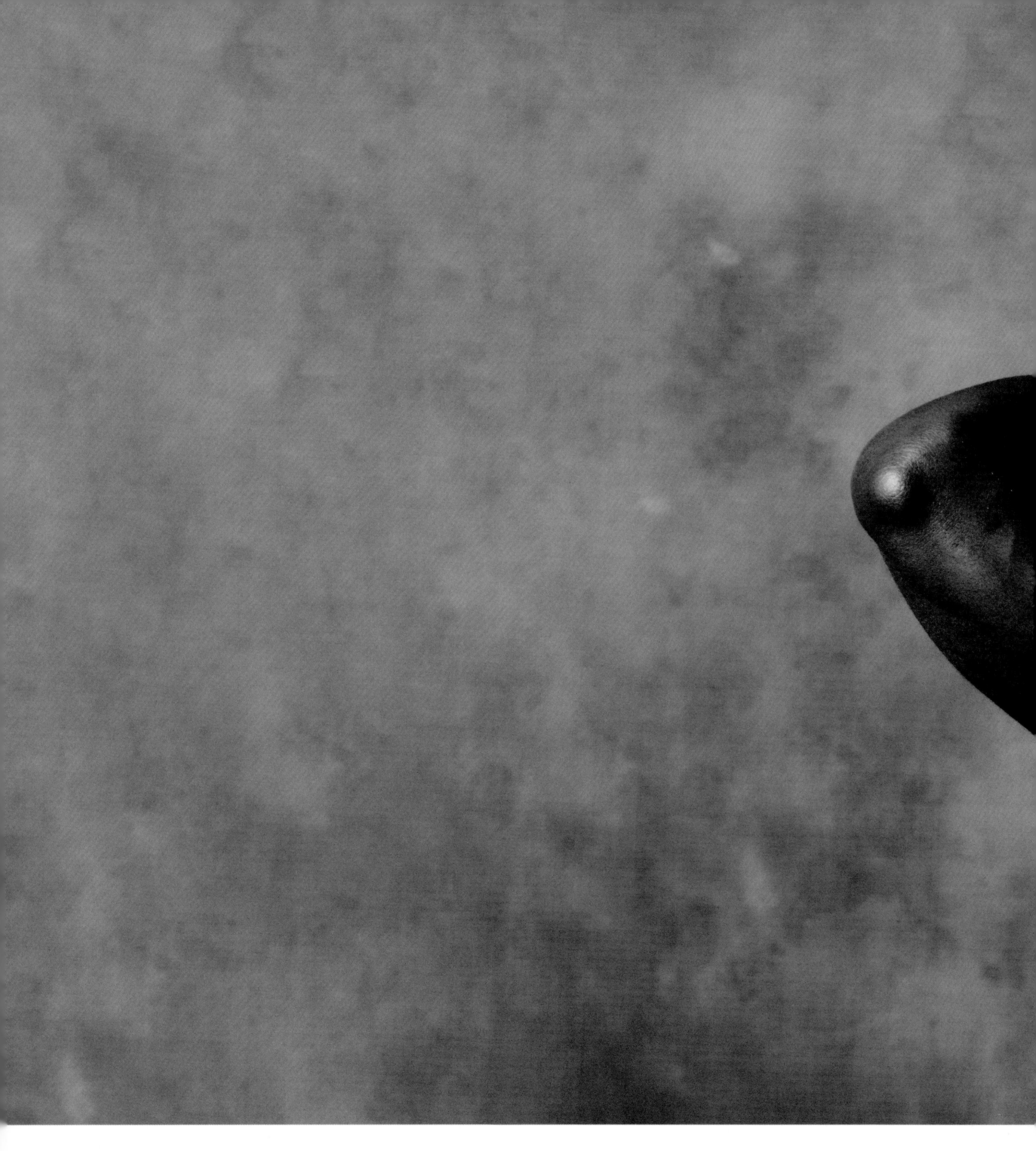

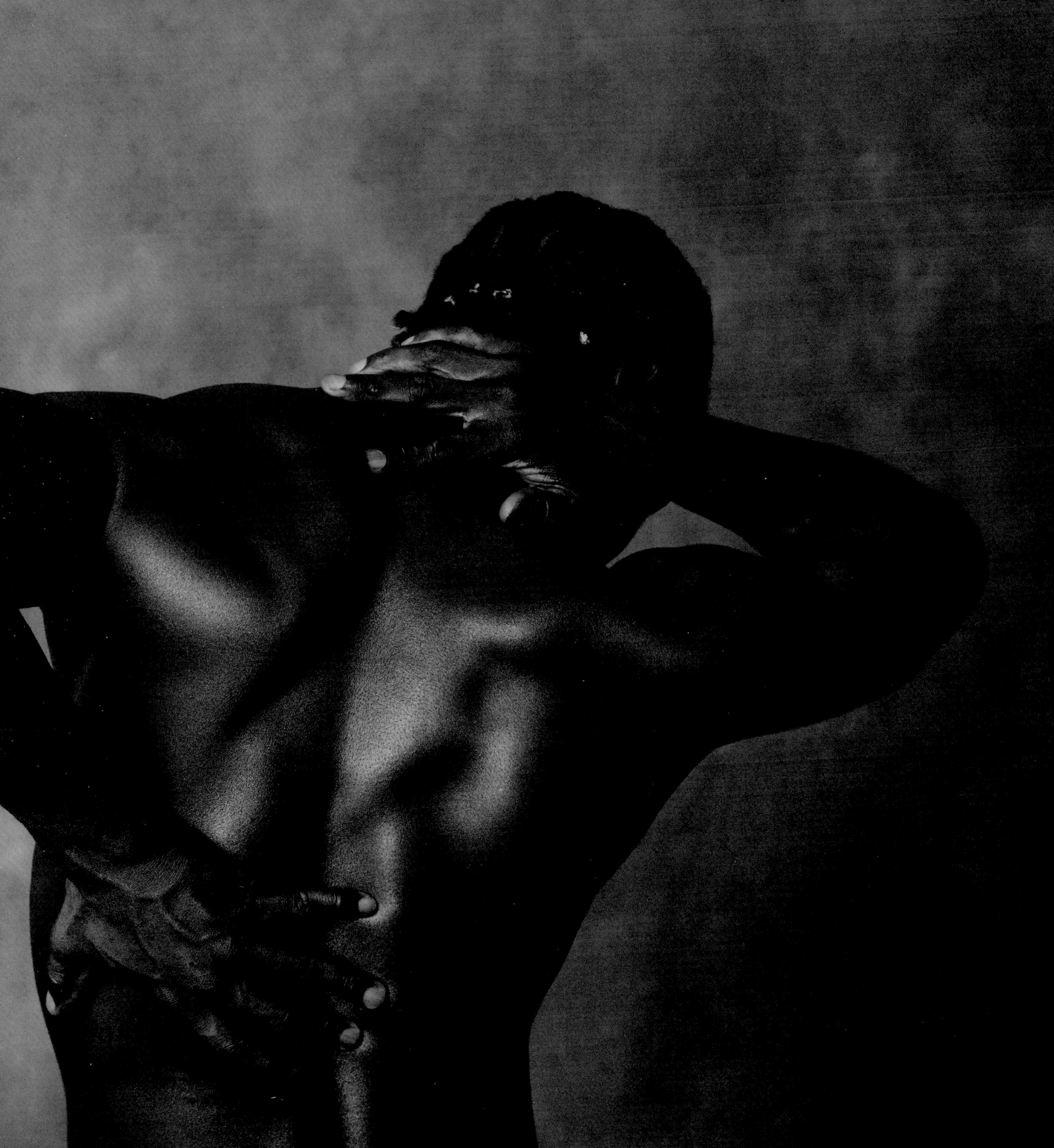

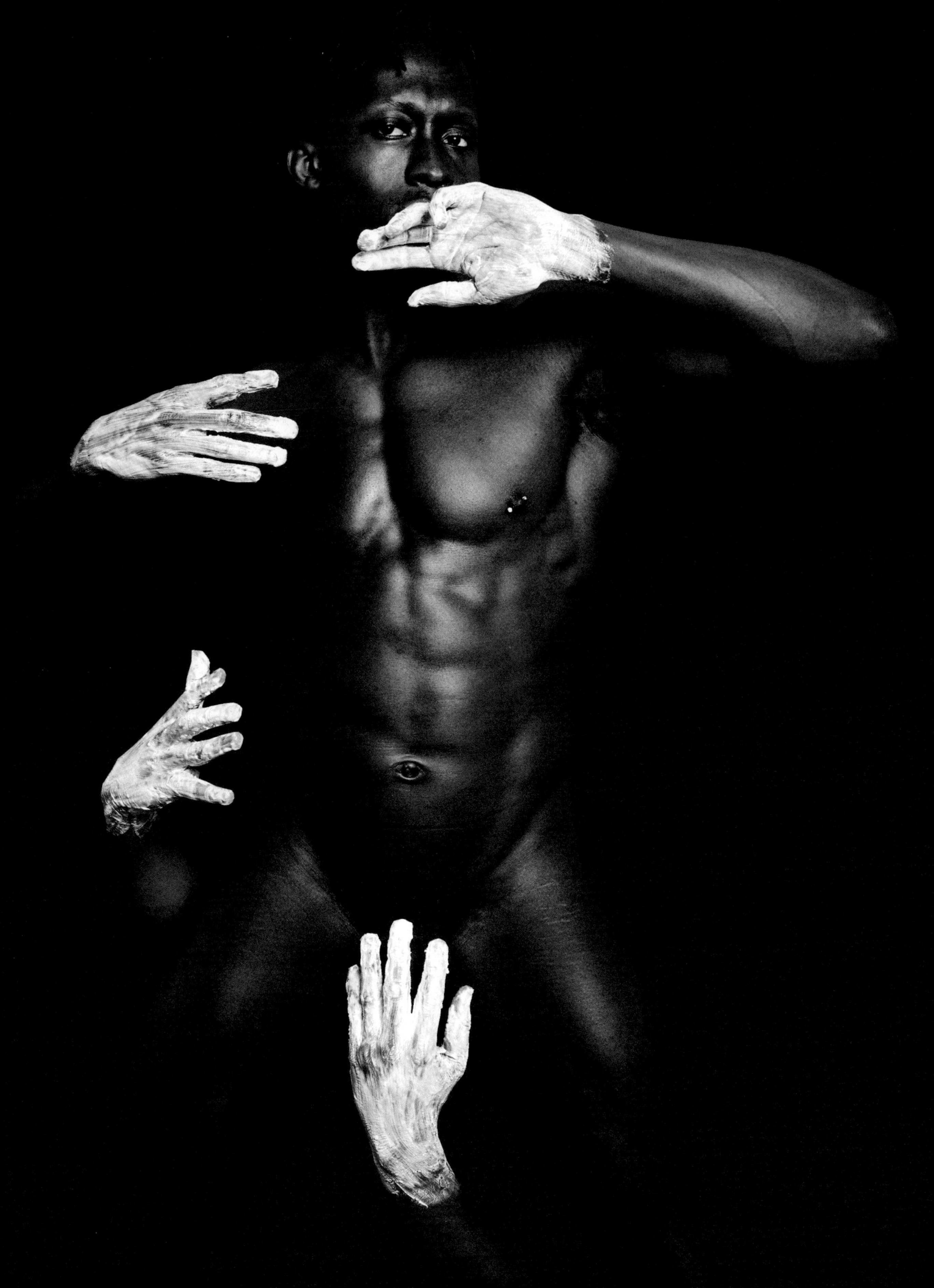

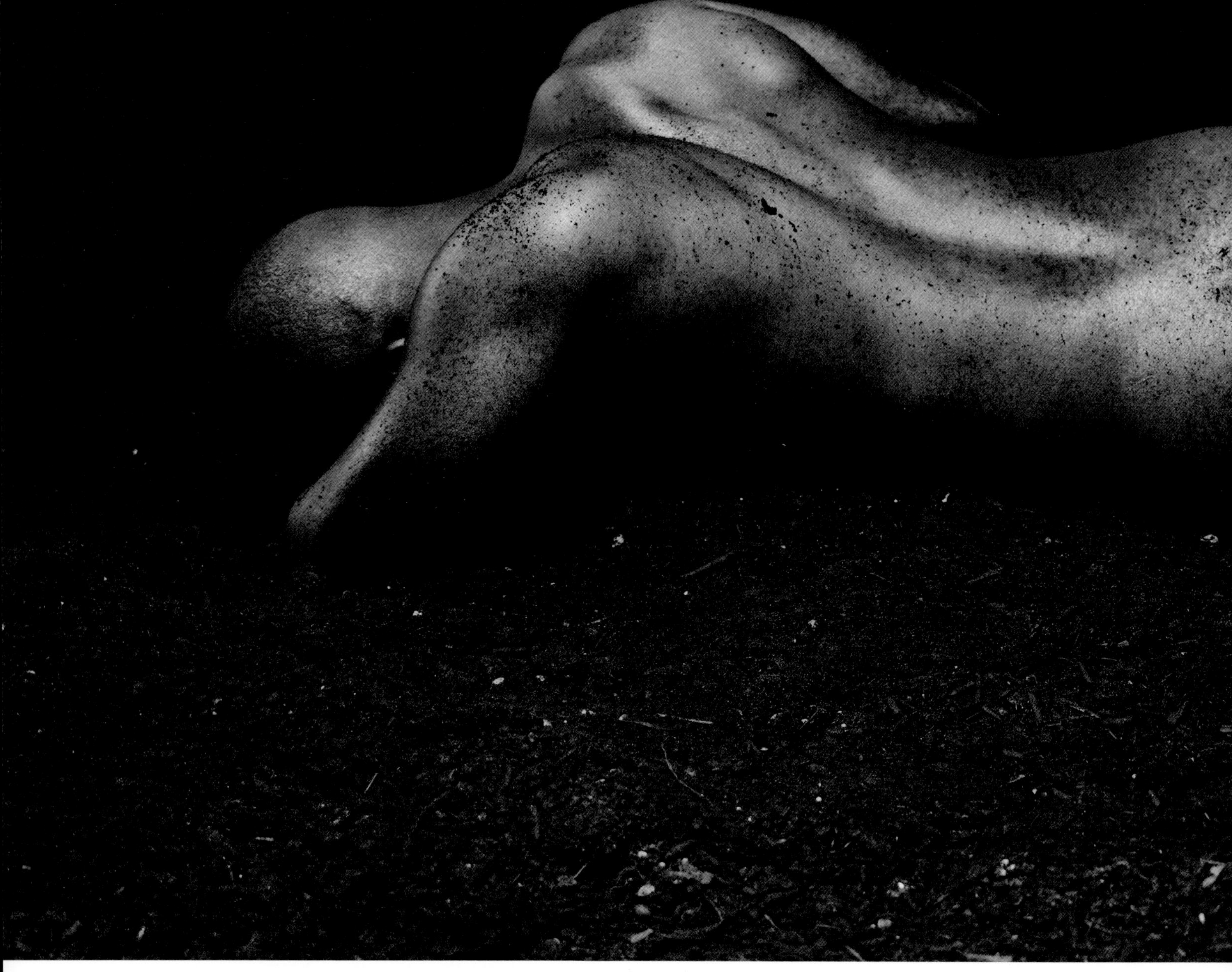

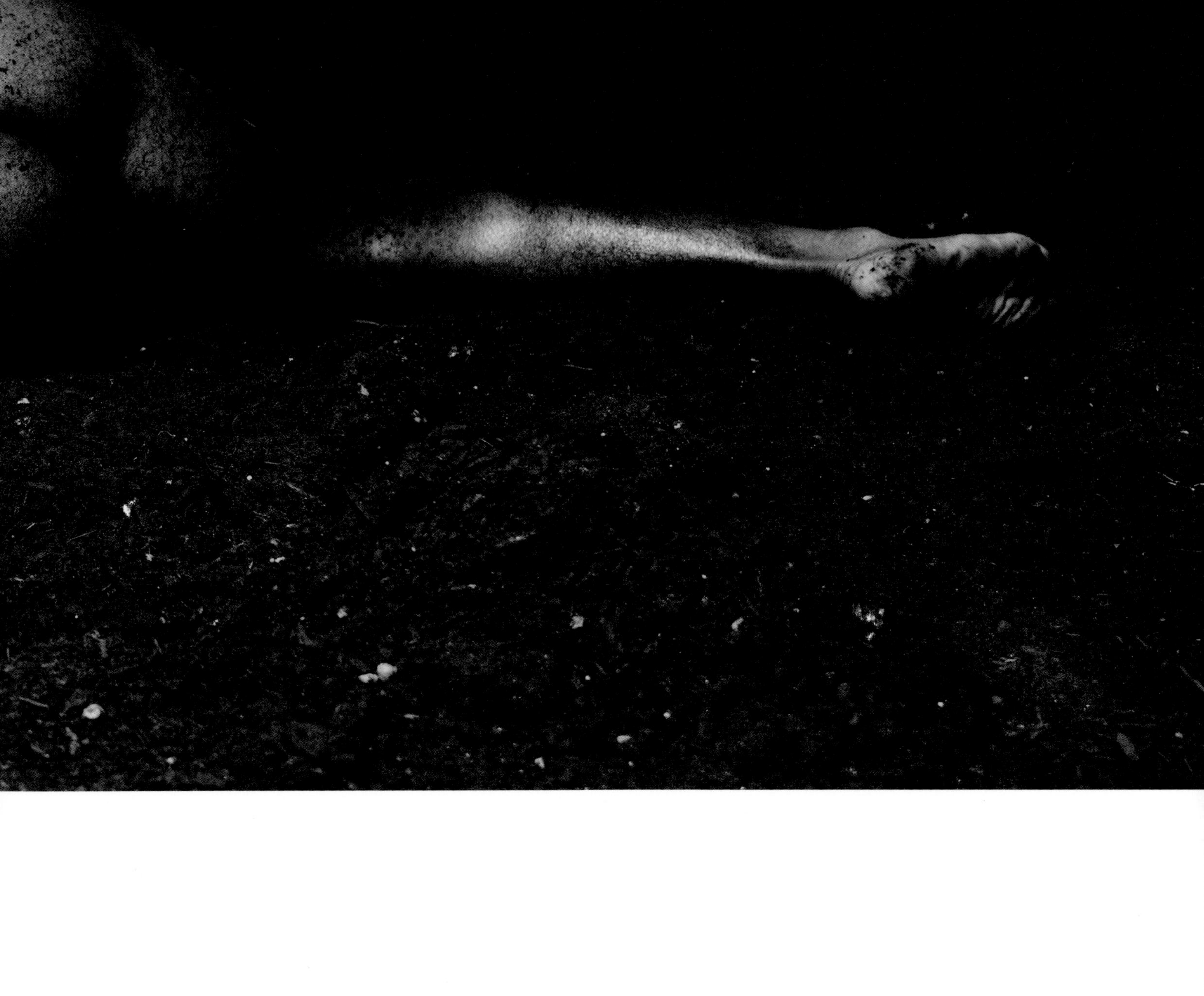

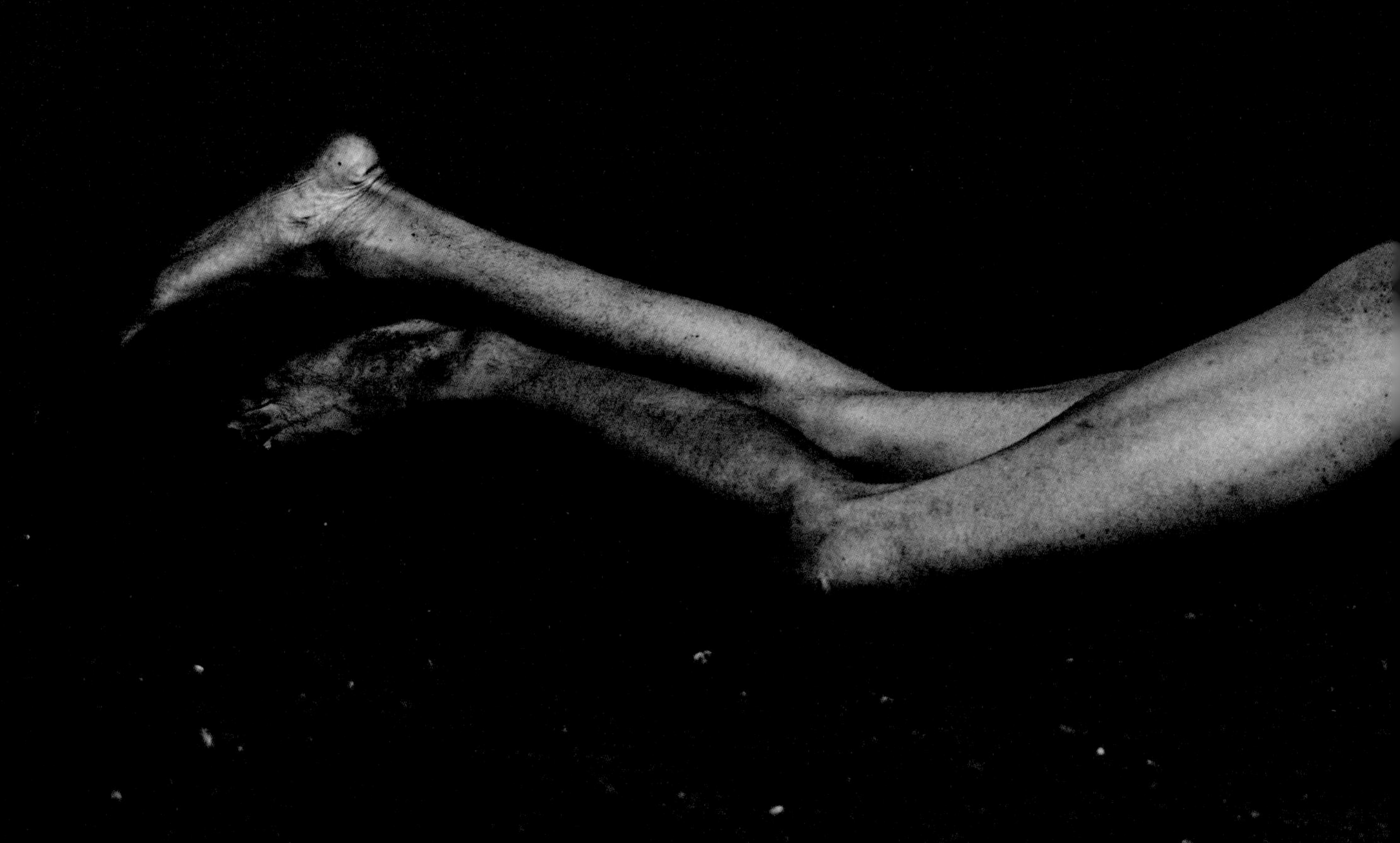

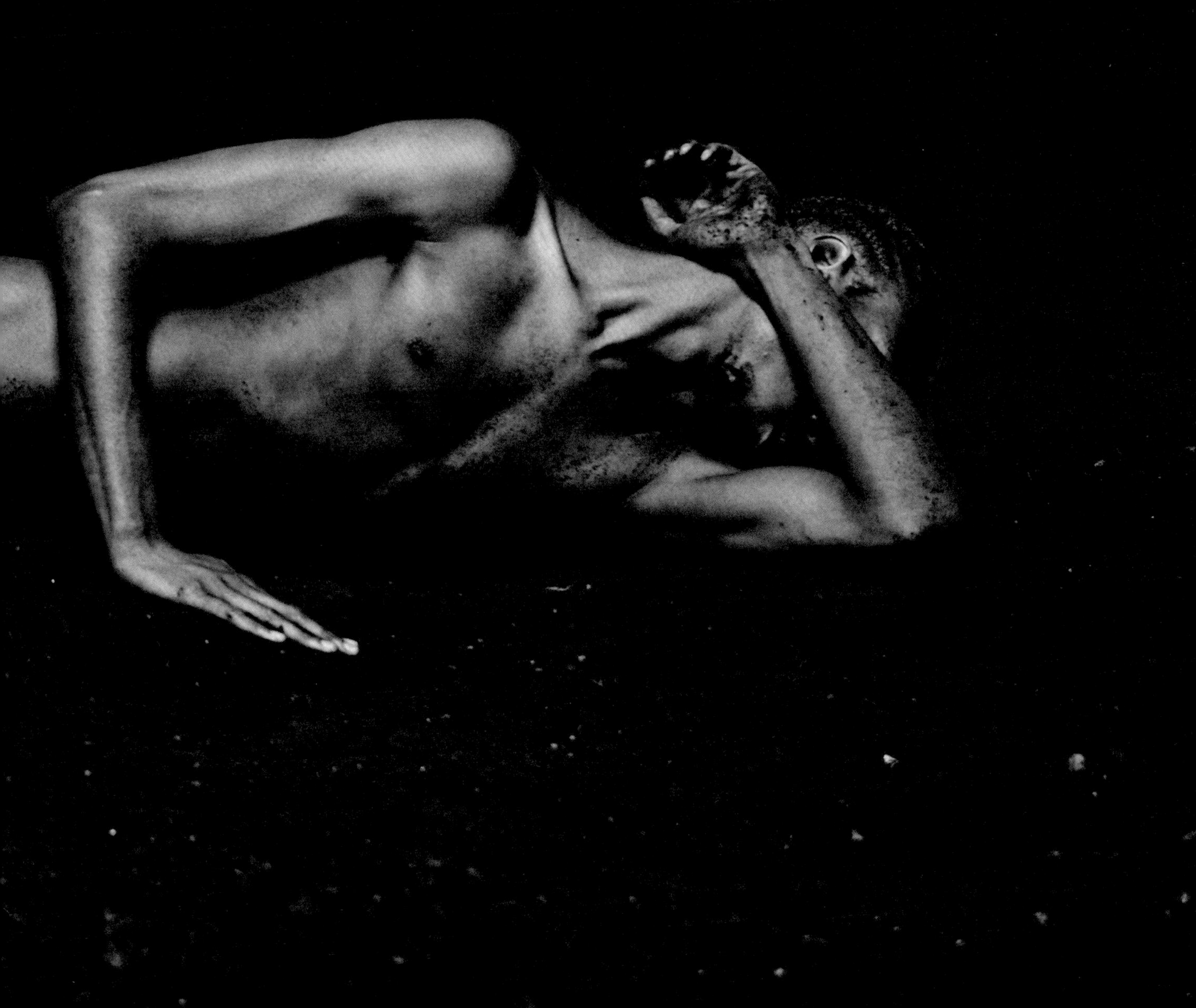

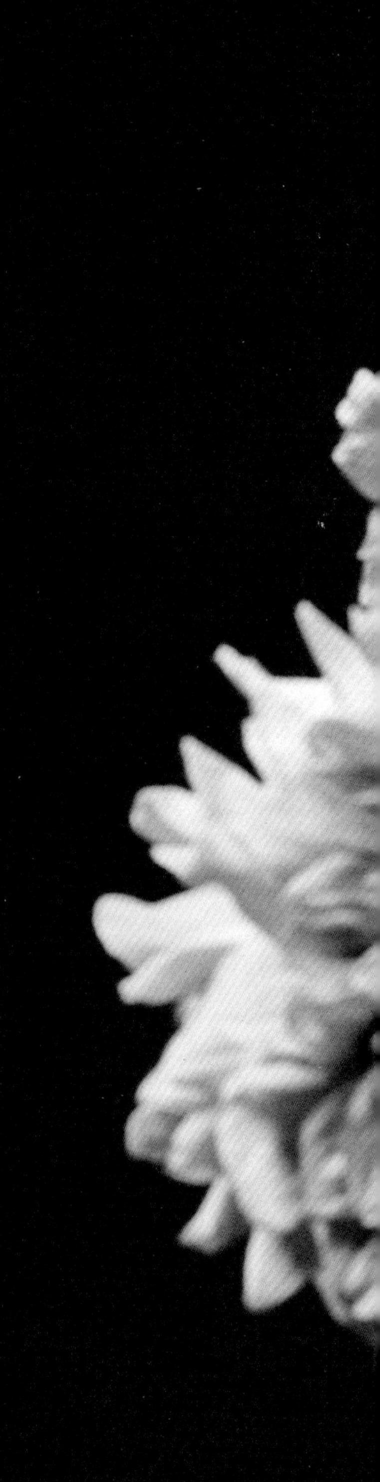

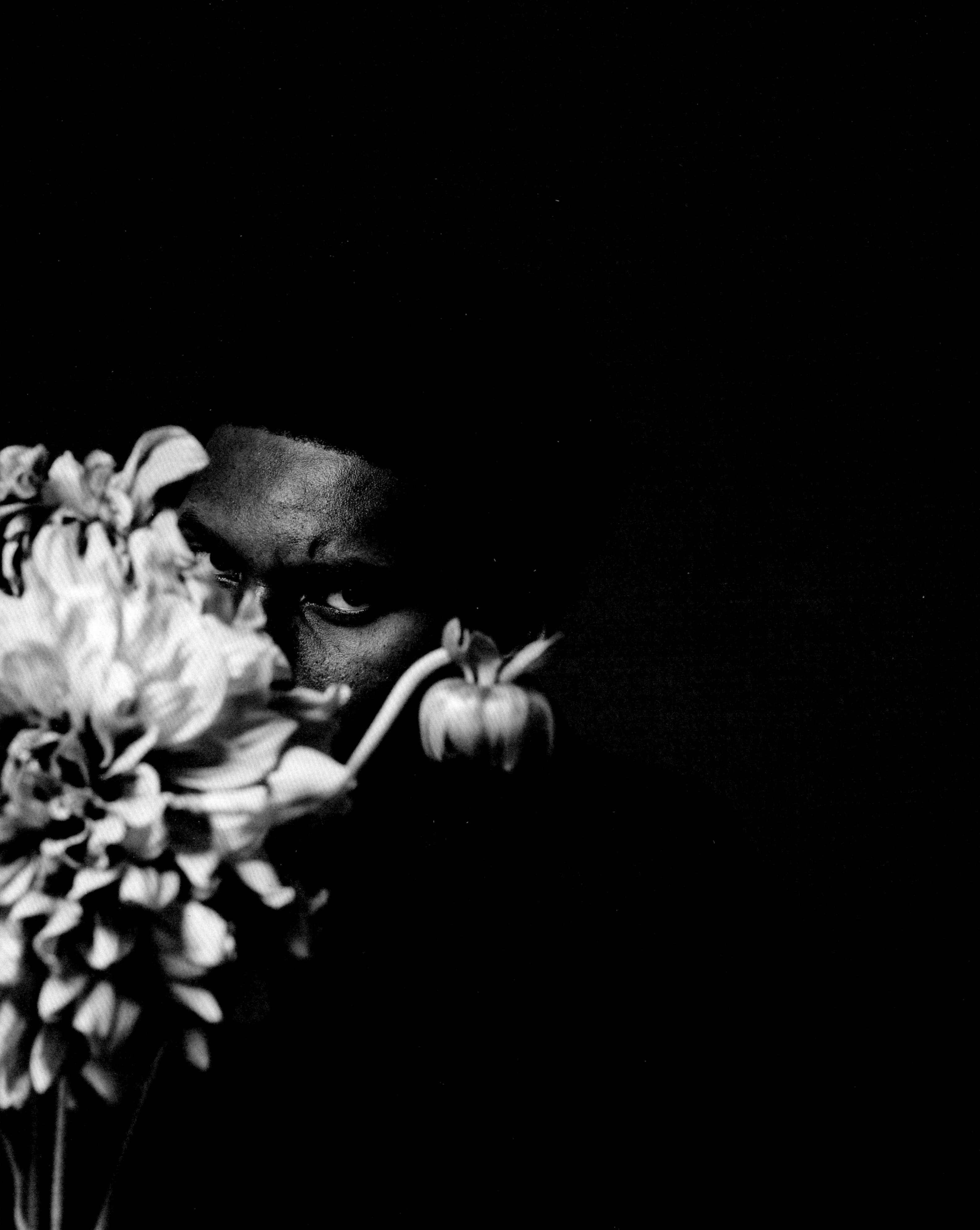

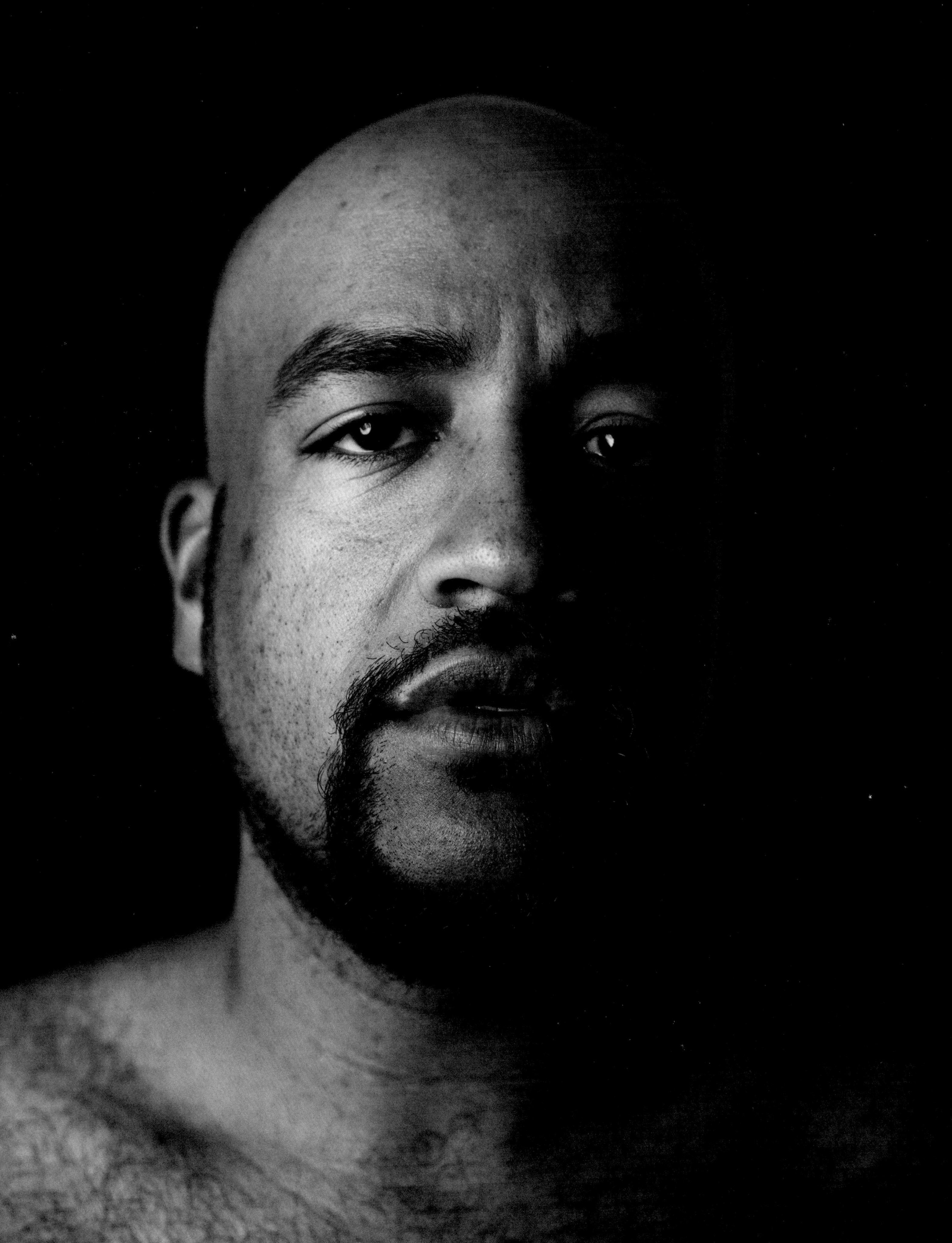

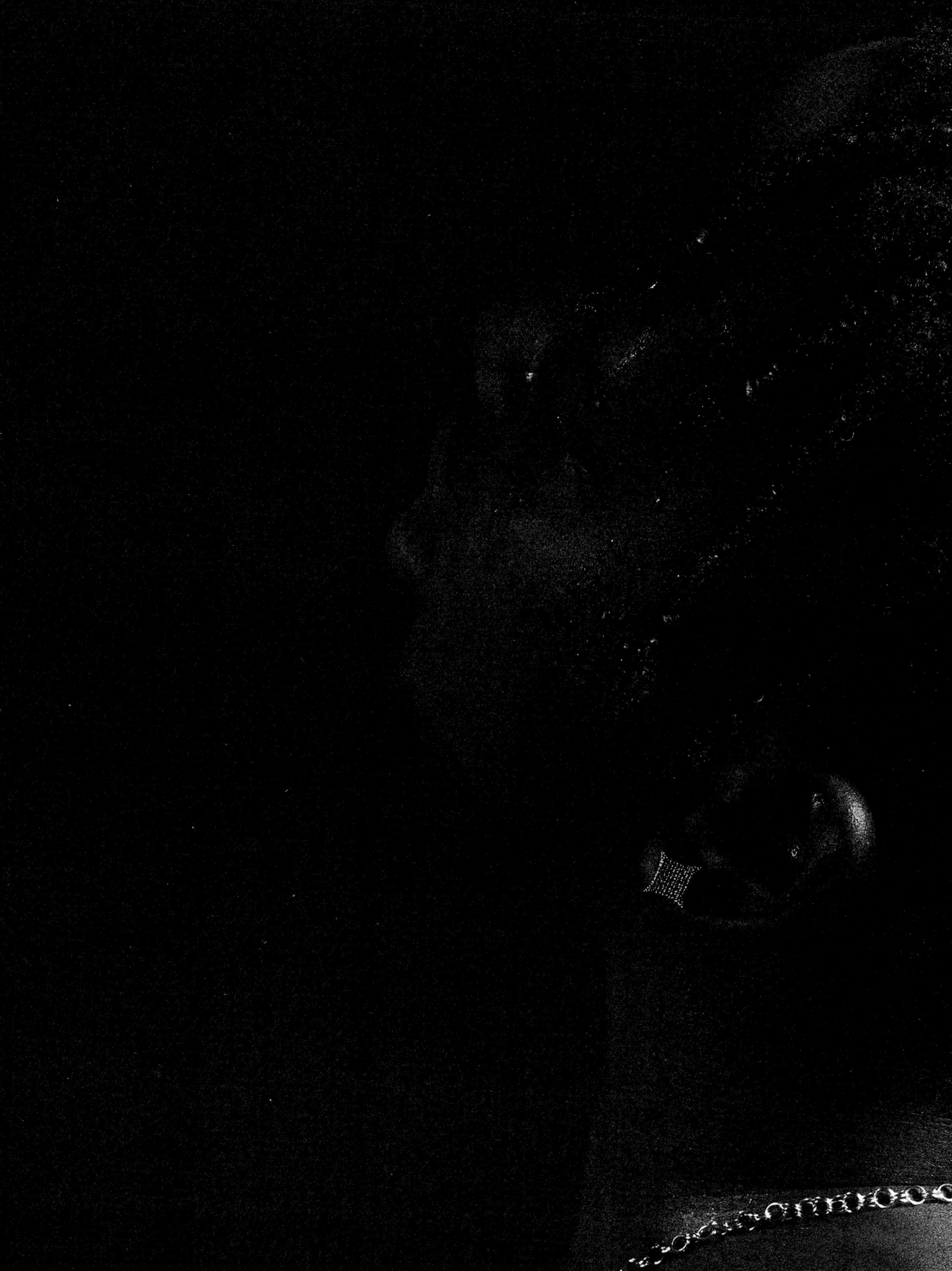

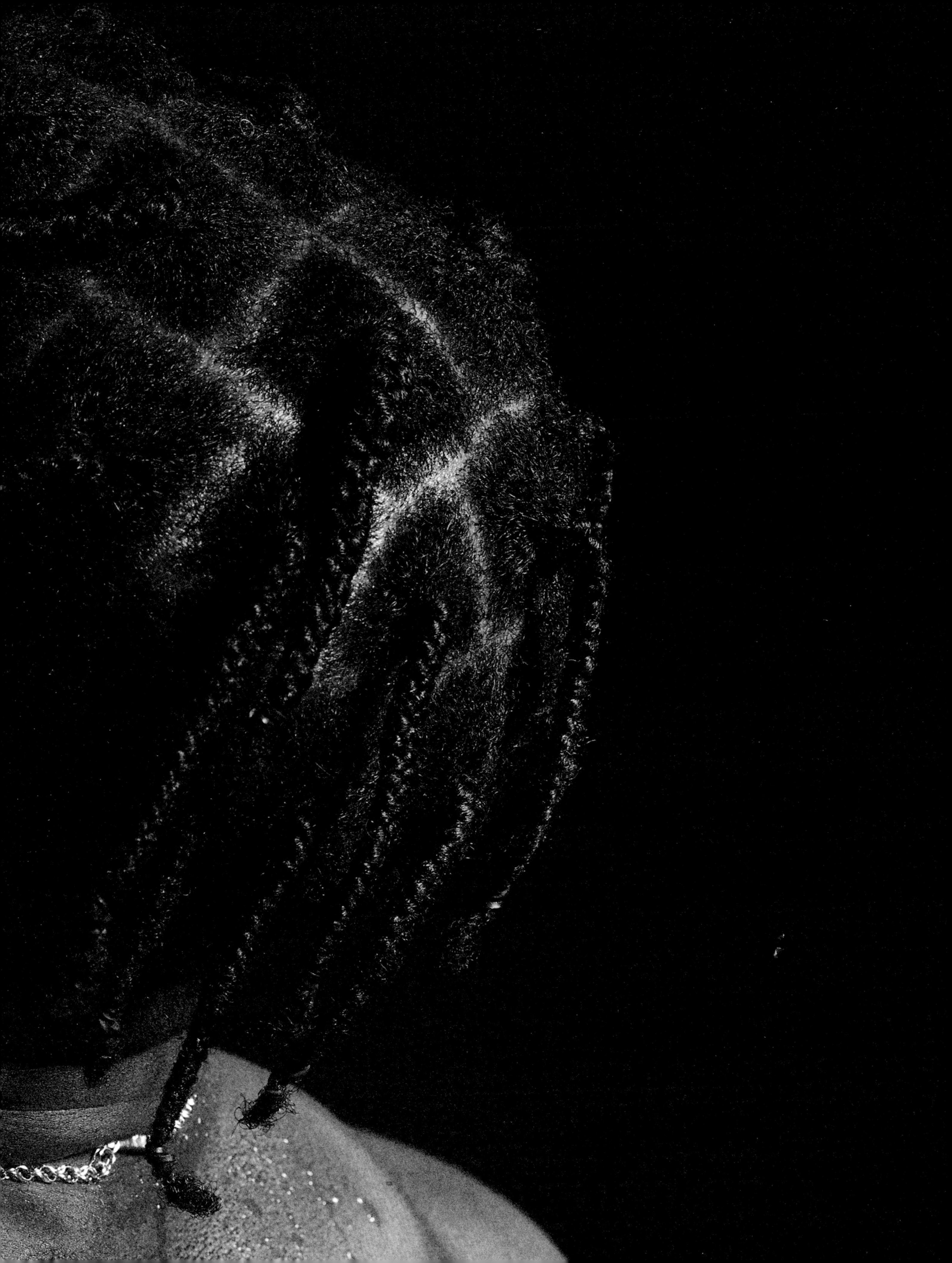

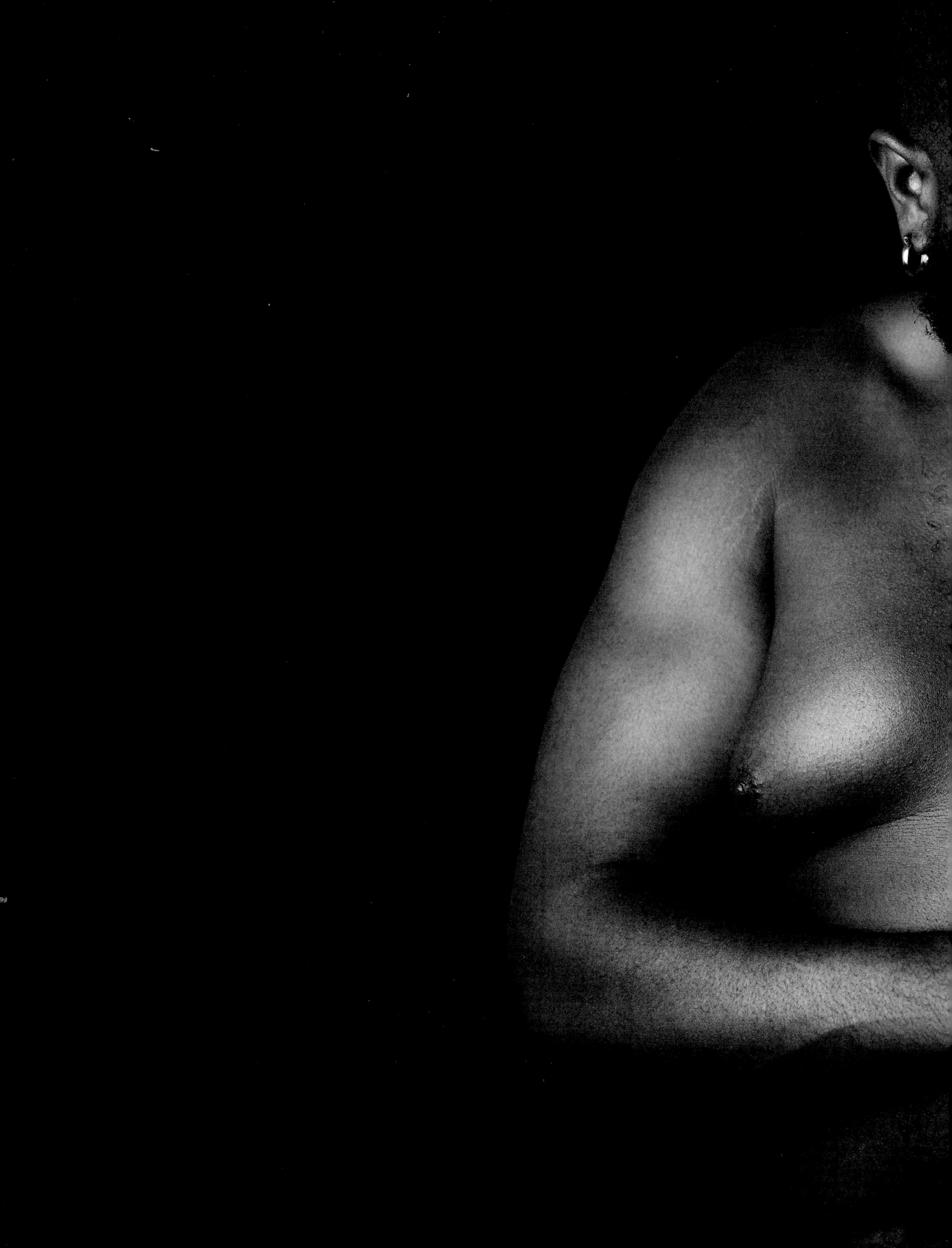

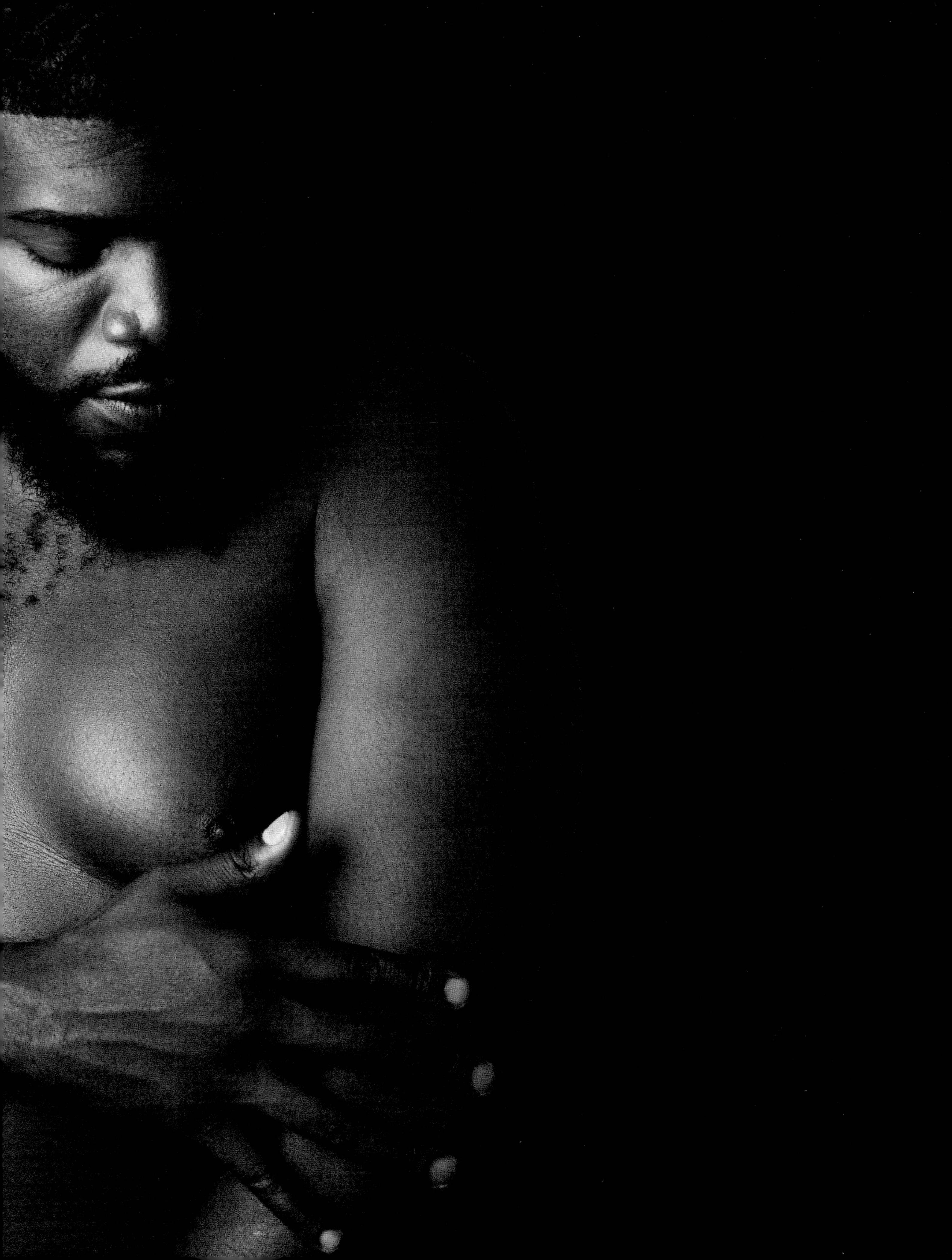

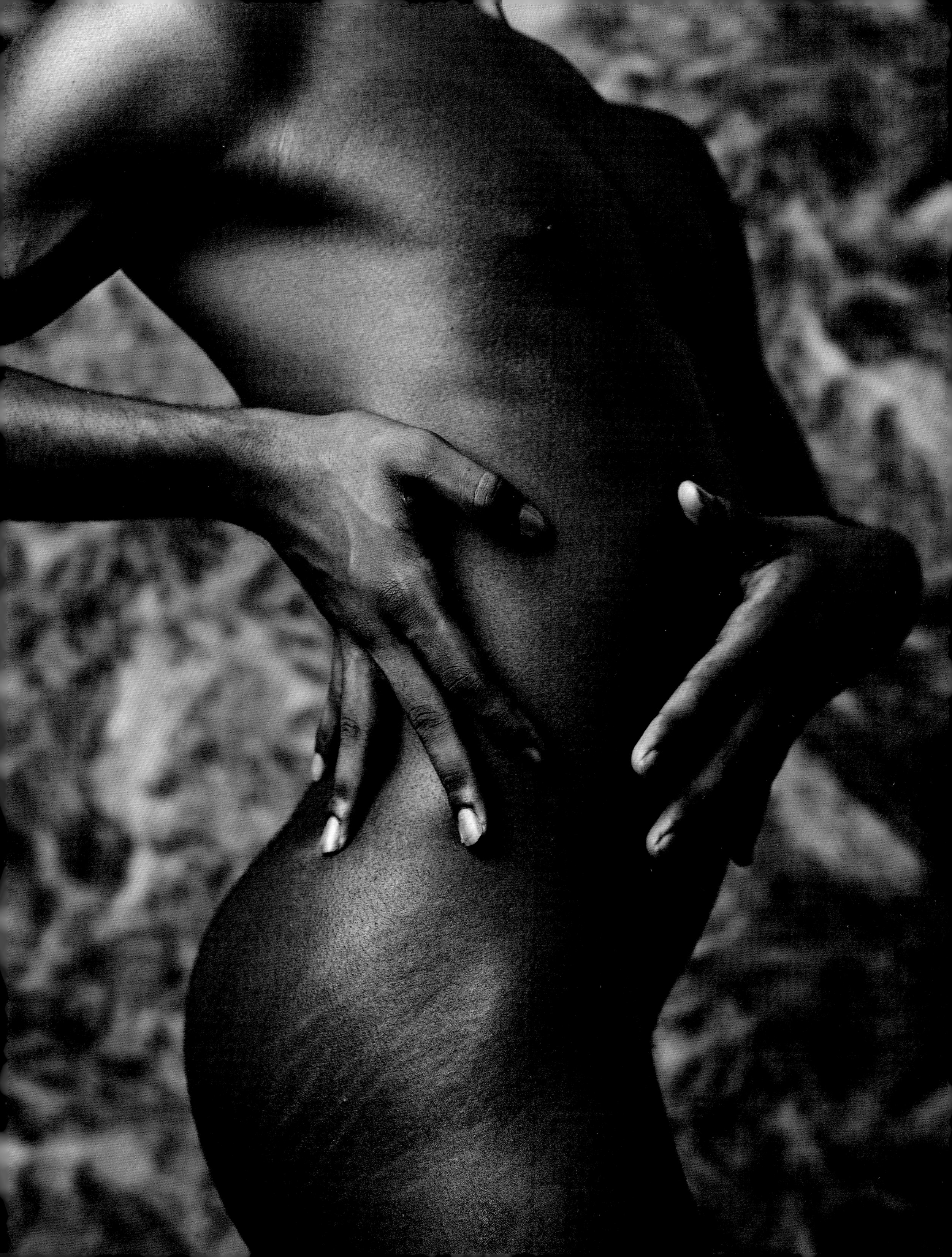

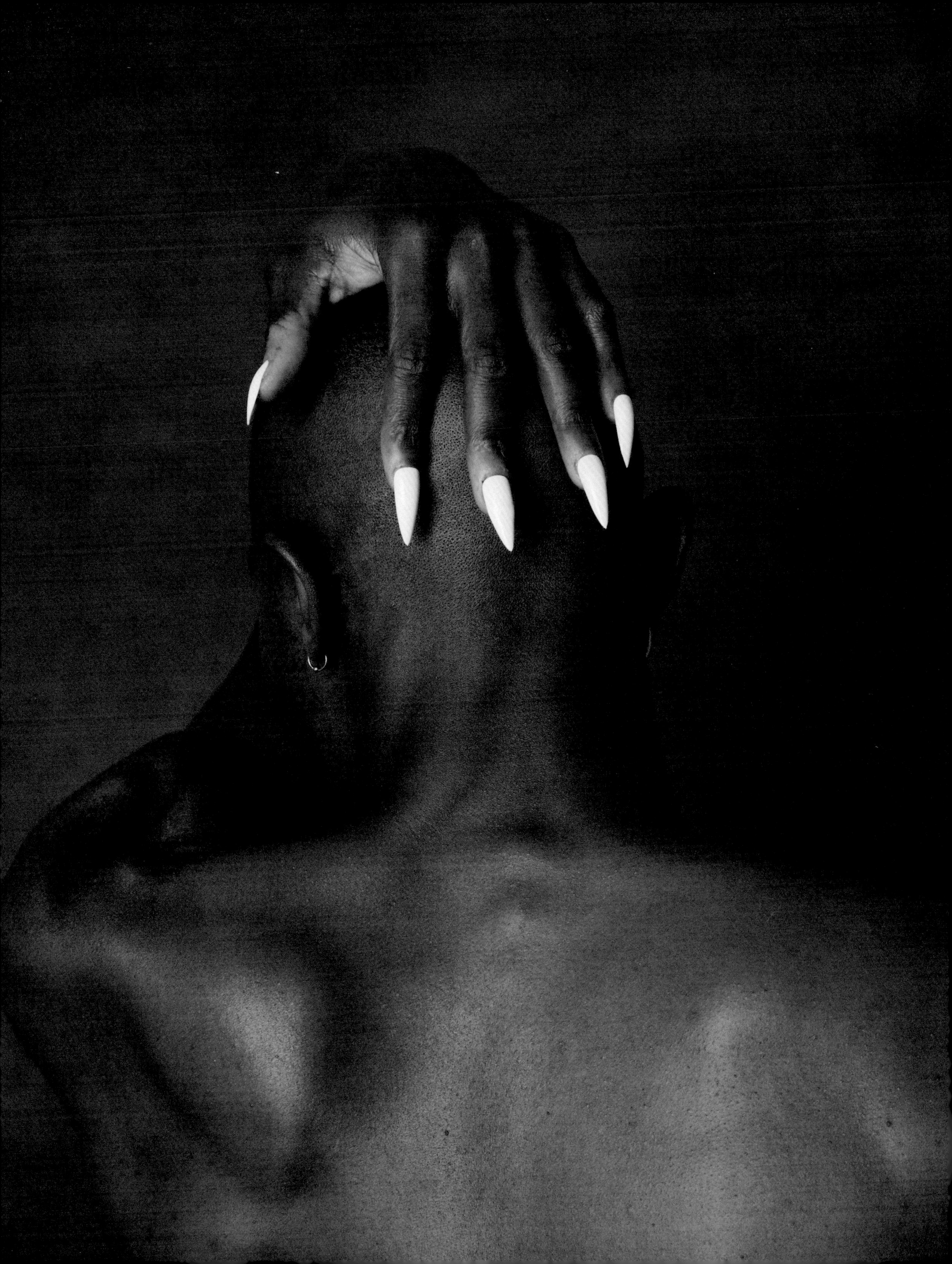

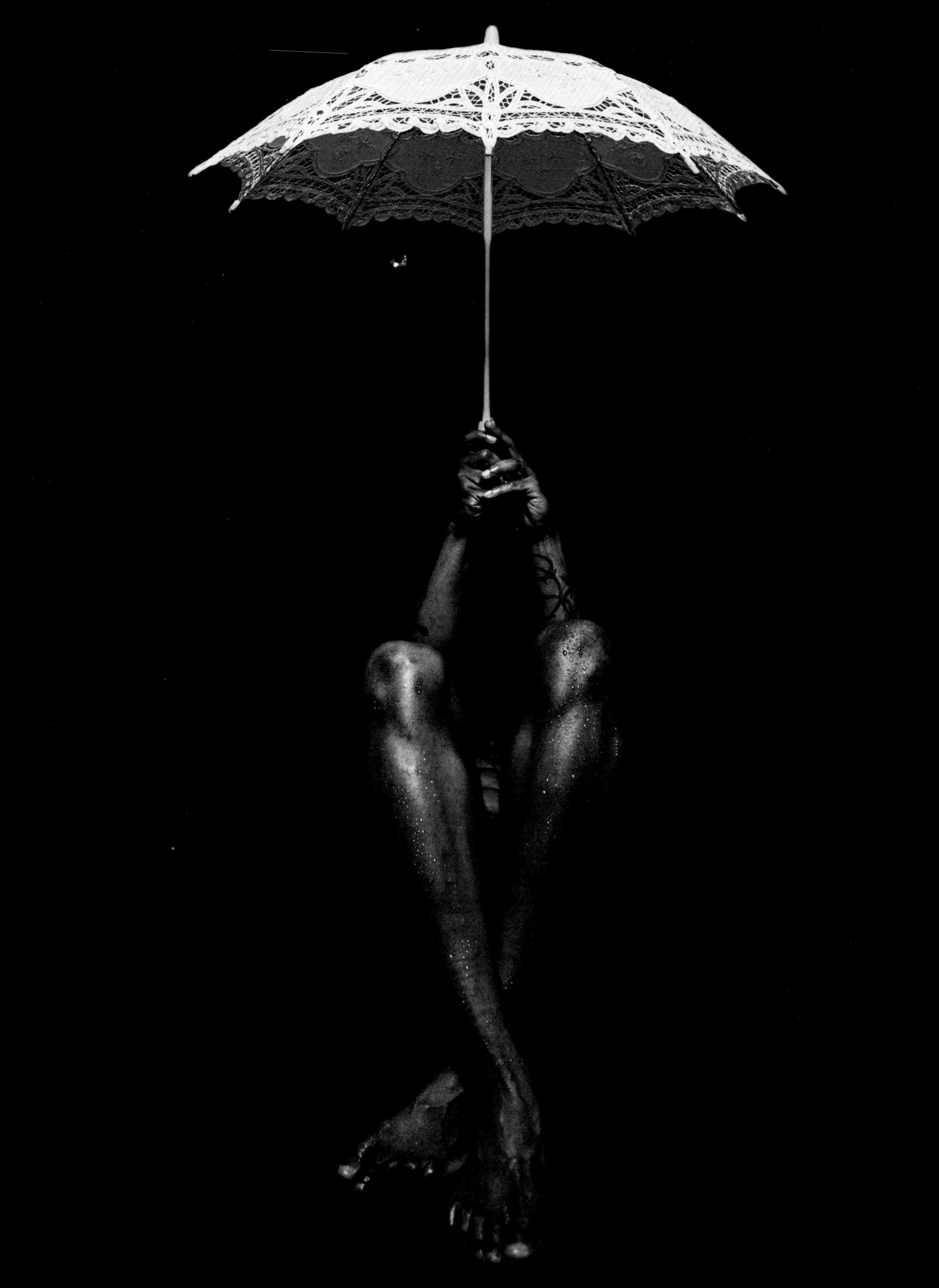

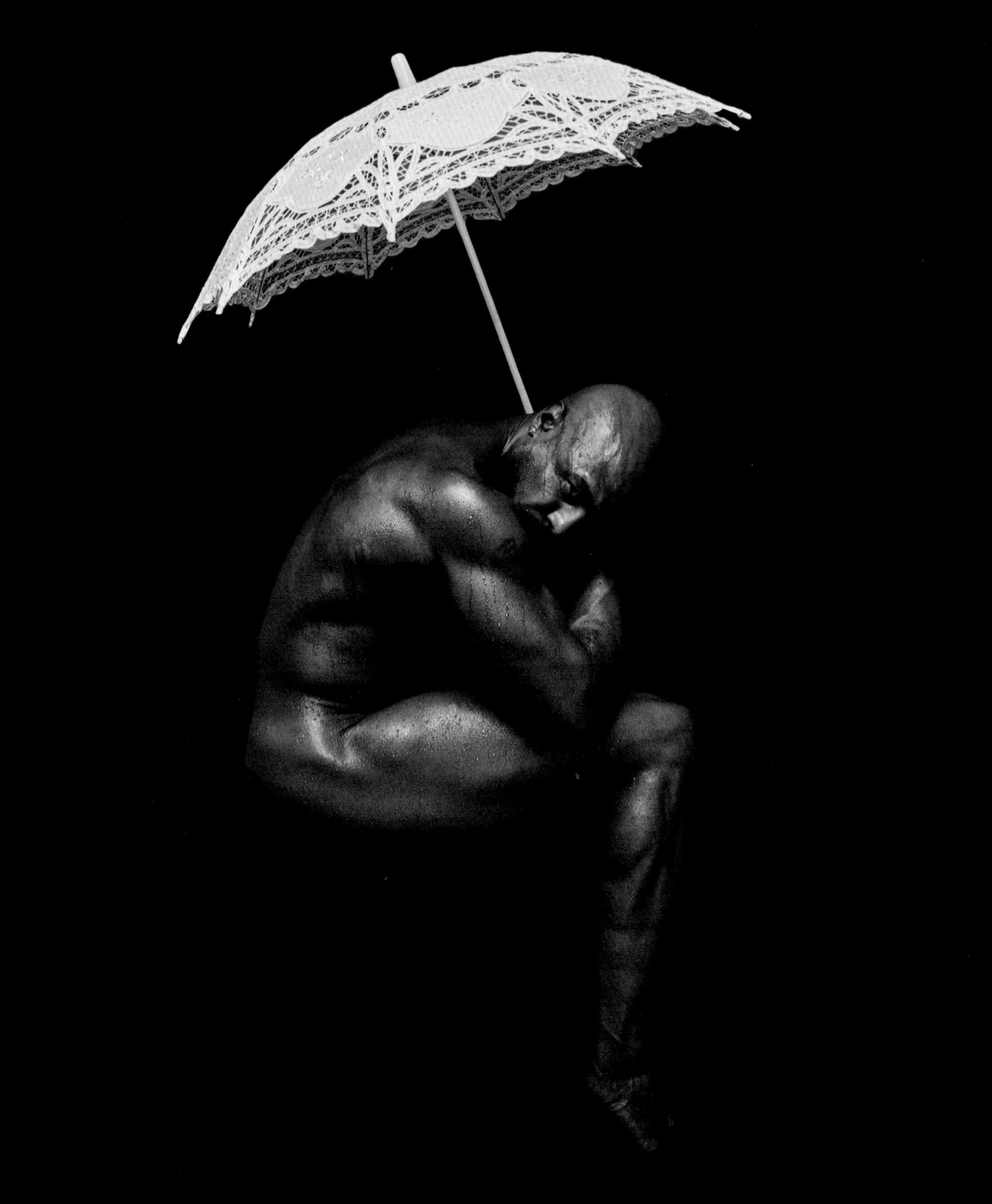

“WE NEED IN EVERY COMMUNITY, A GROUP OF
ANGELIC TROUBLEMAKERS”

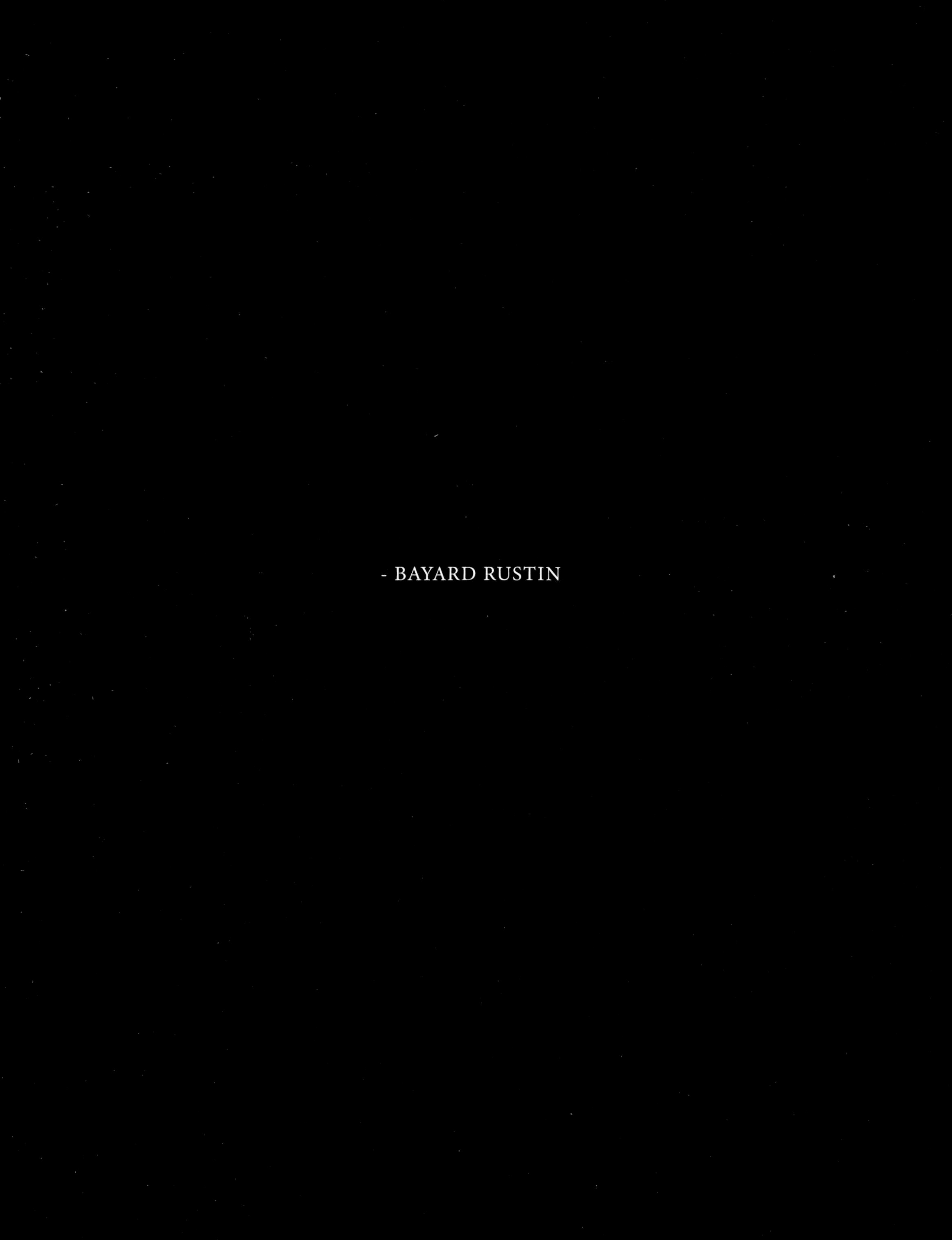
- BAYARD RUSTIN

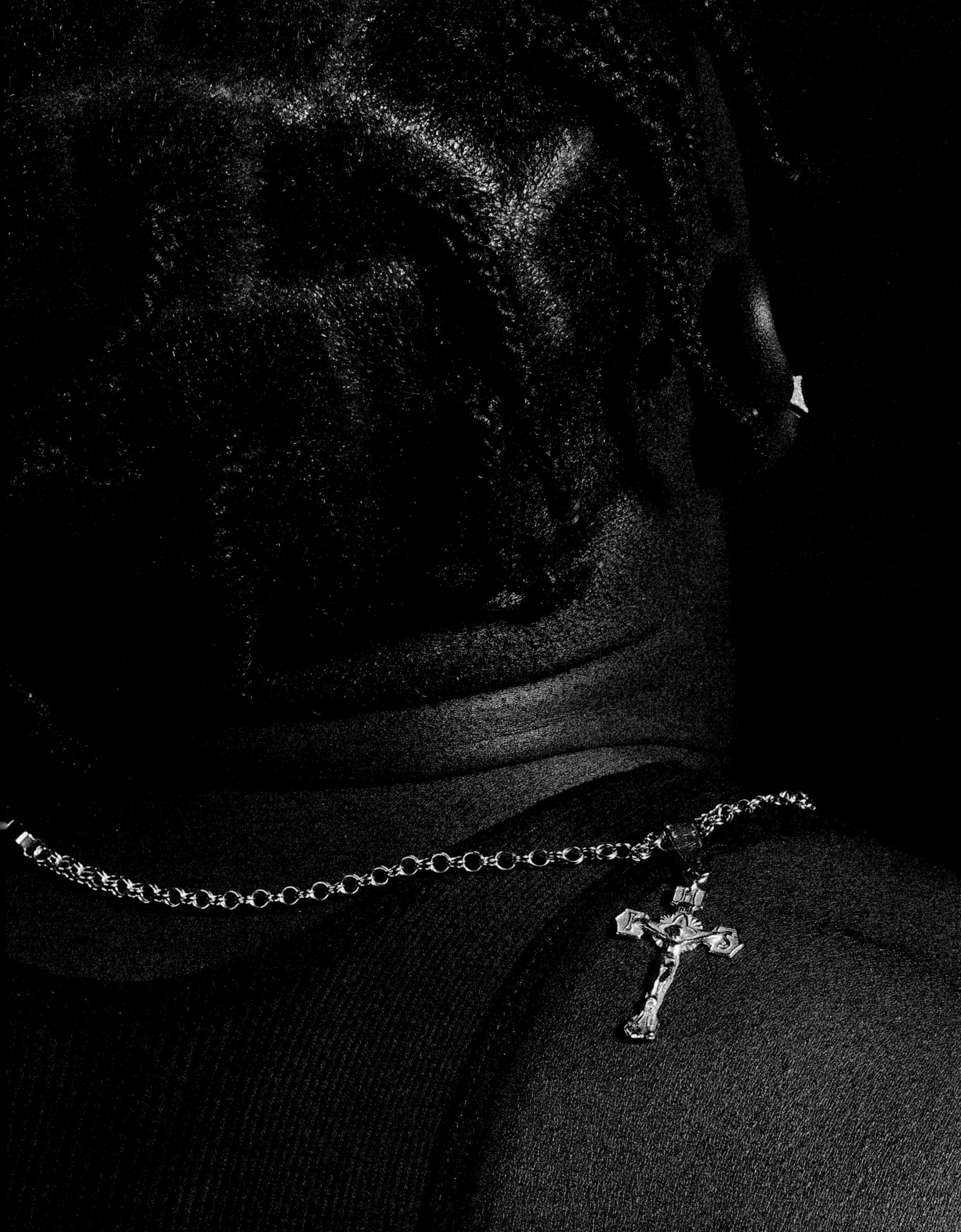

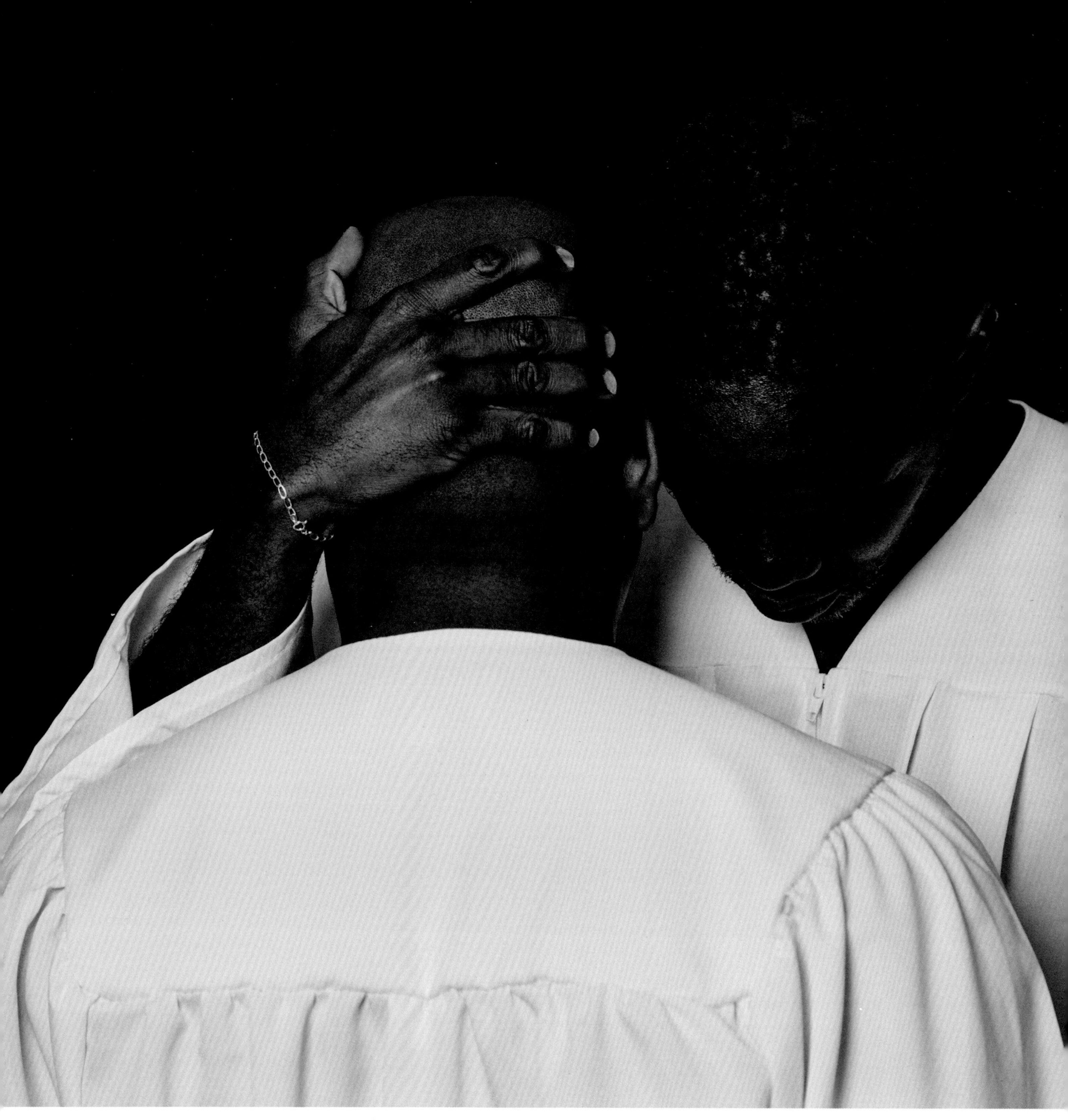

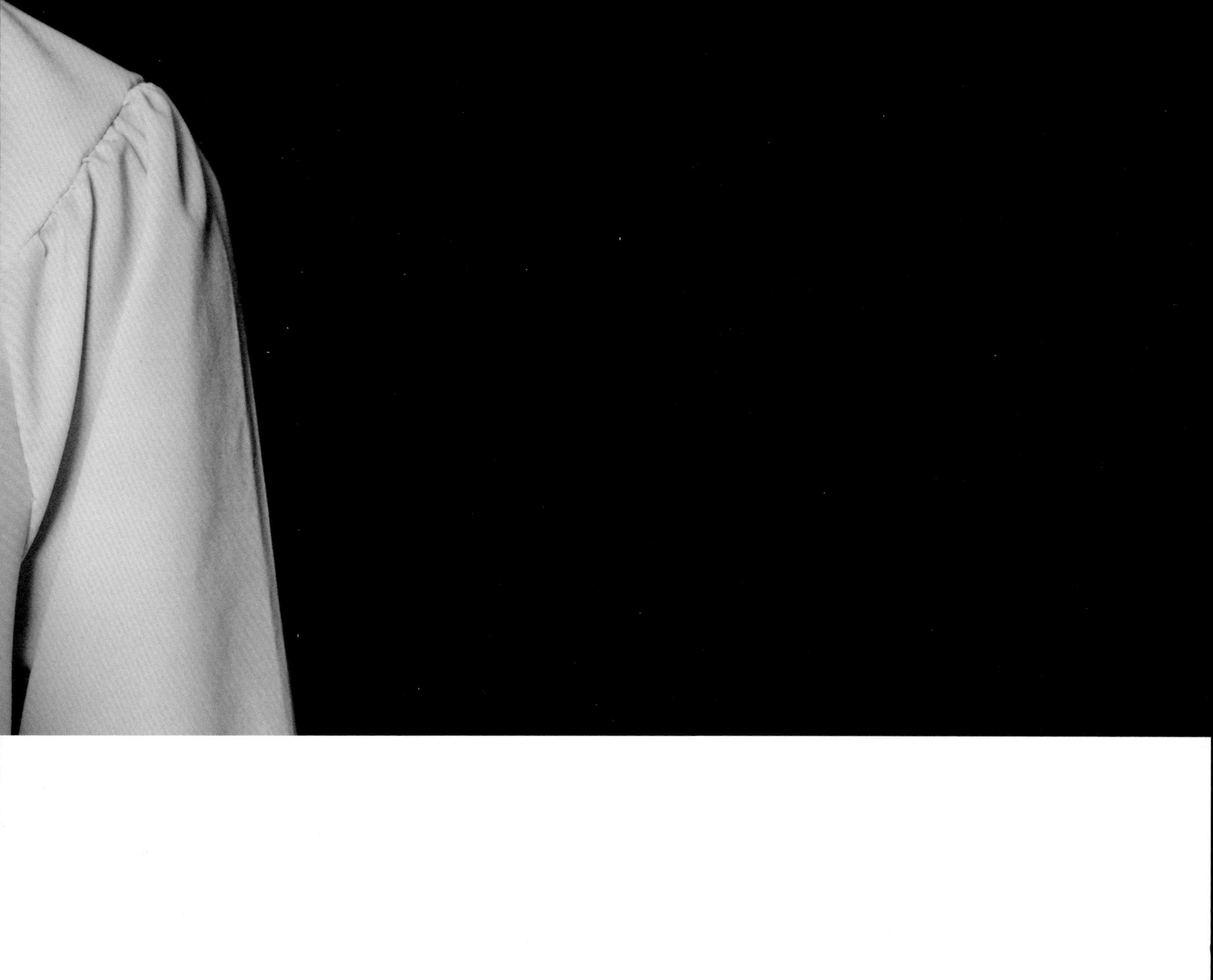

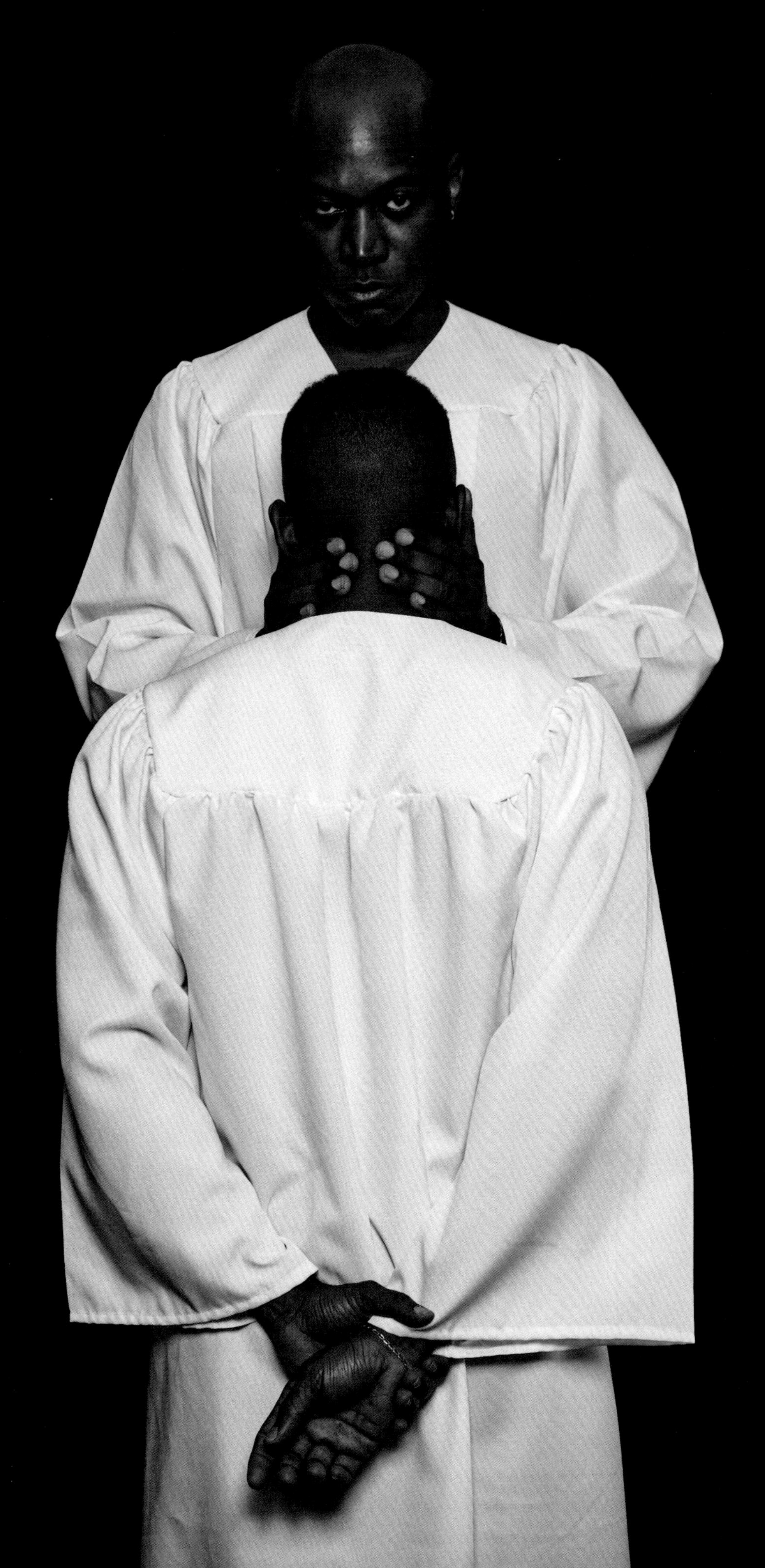

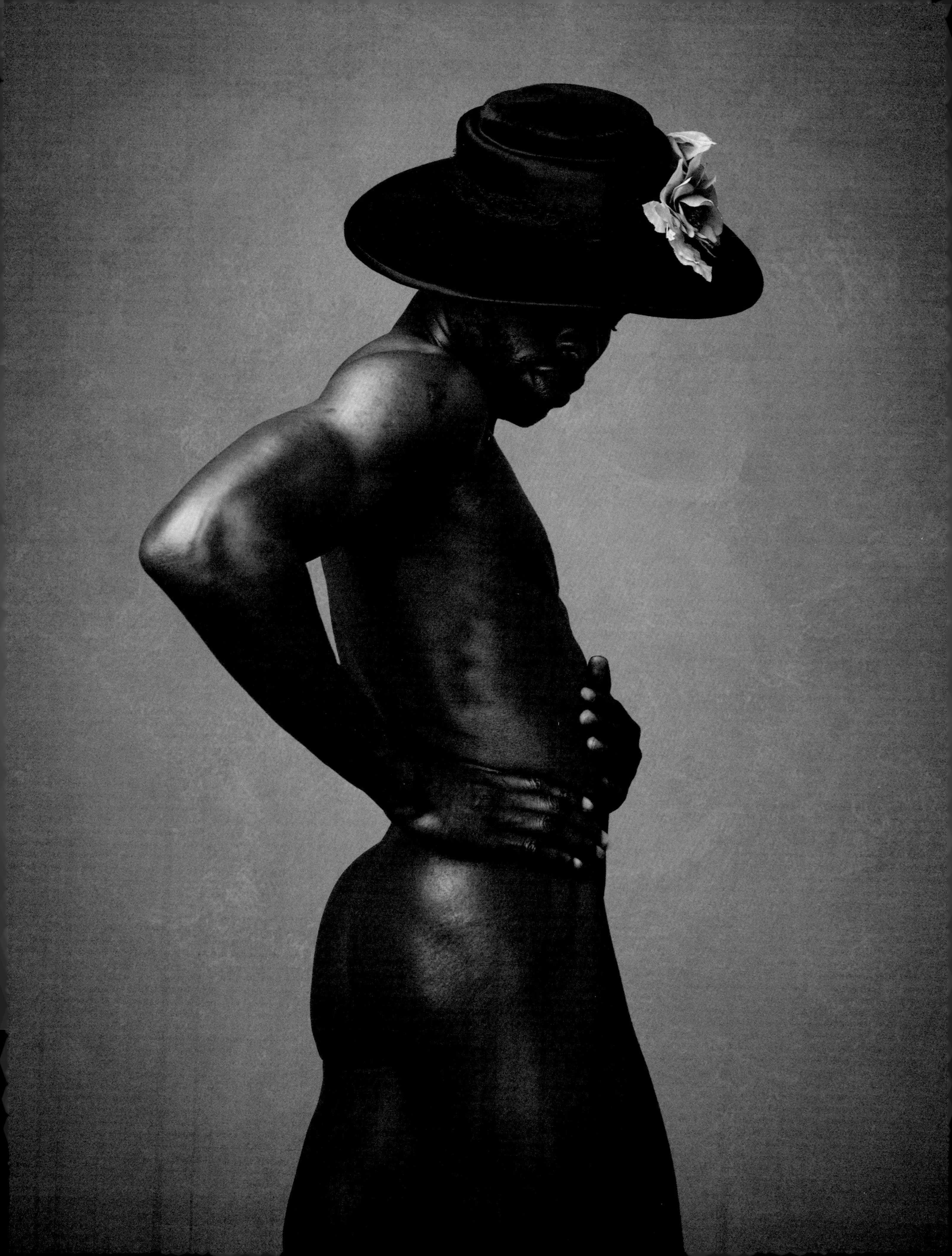

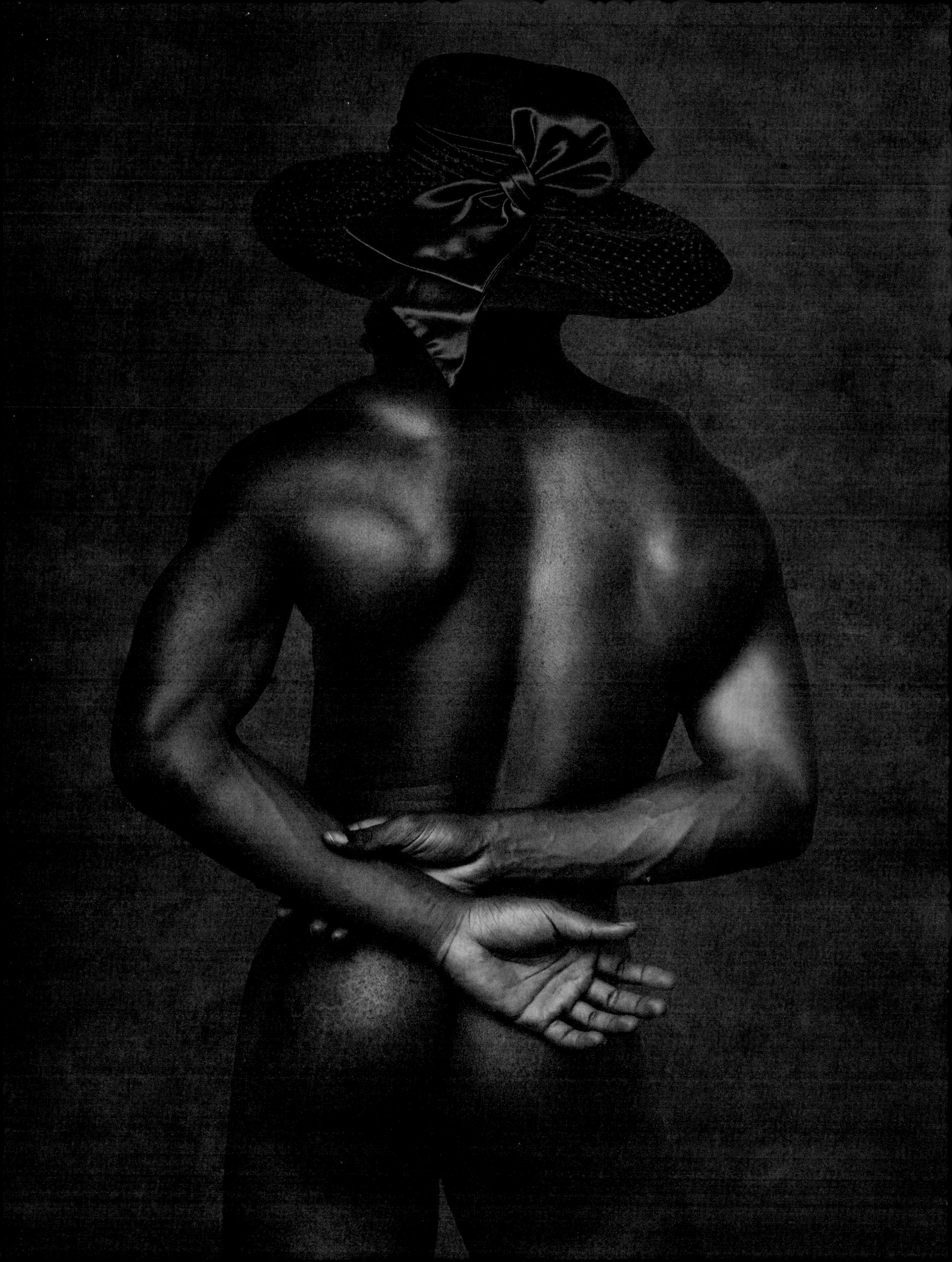

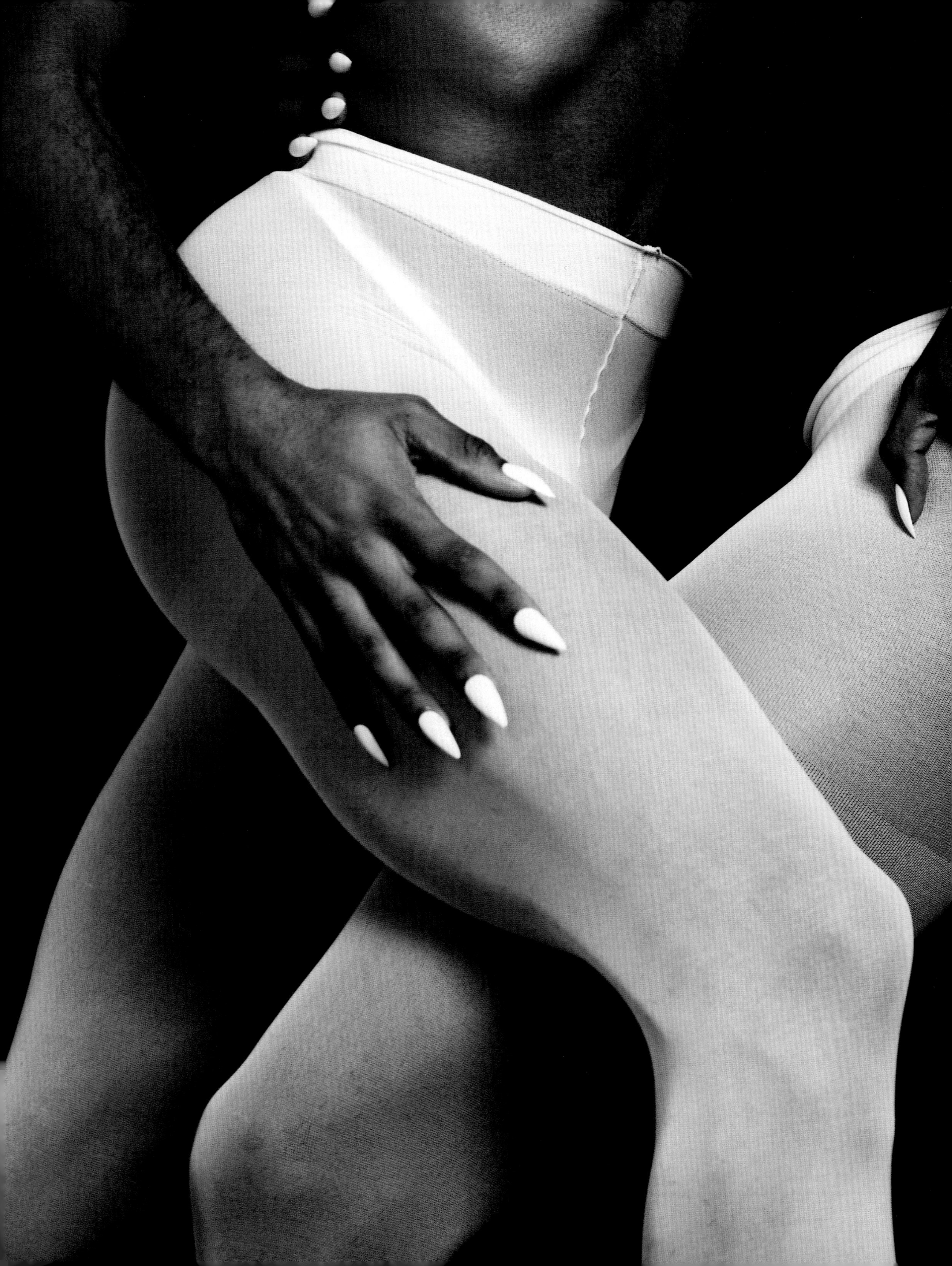

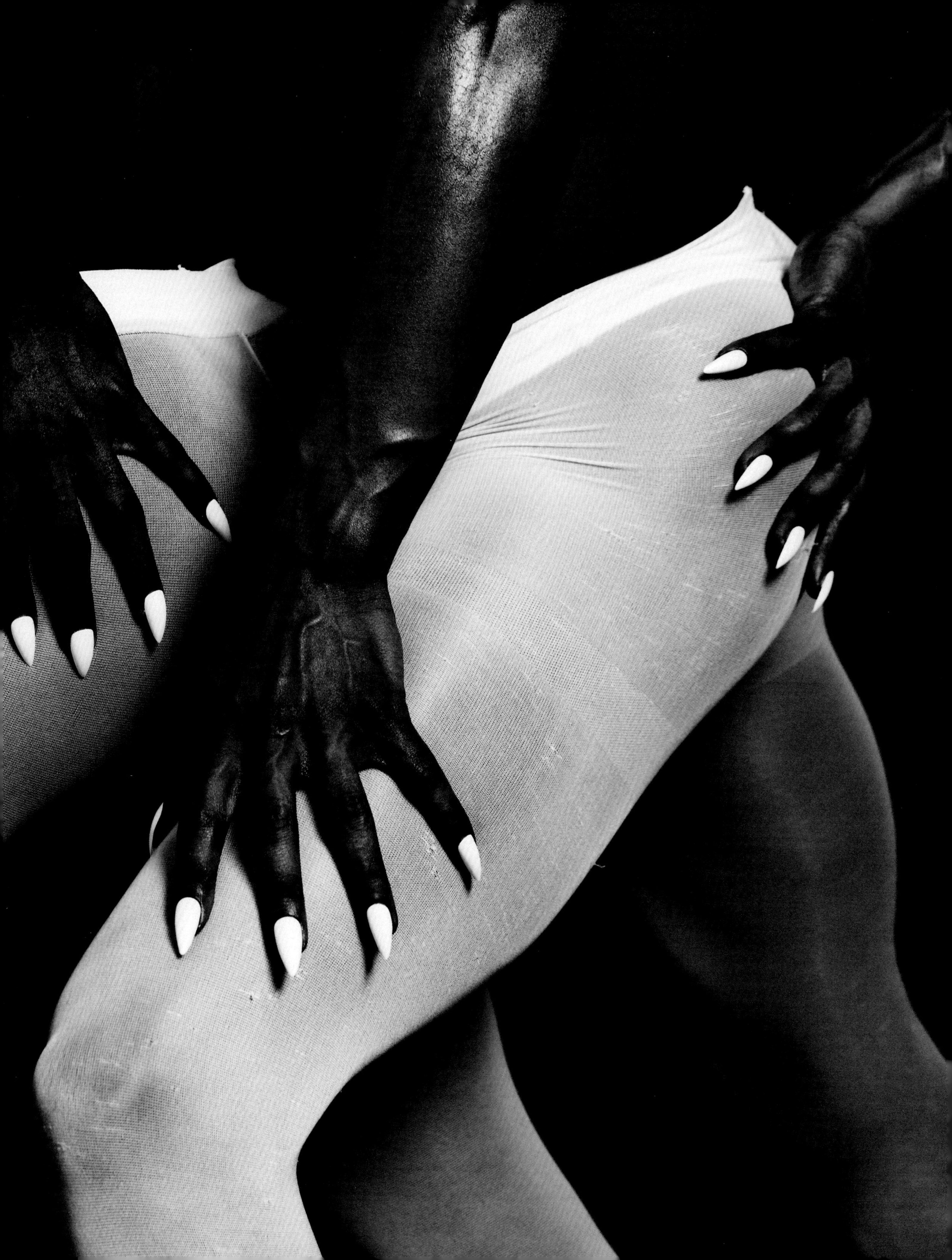

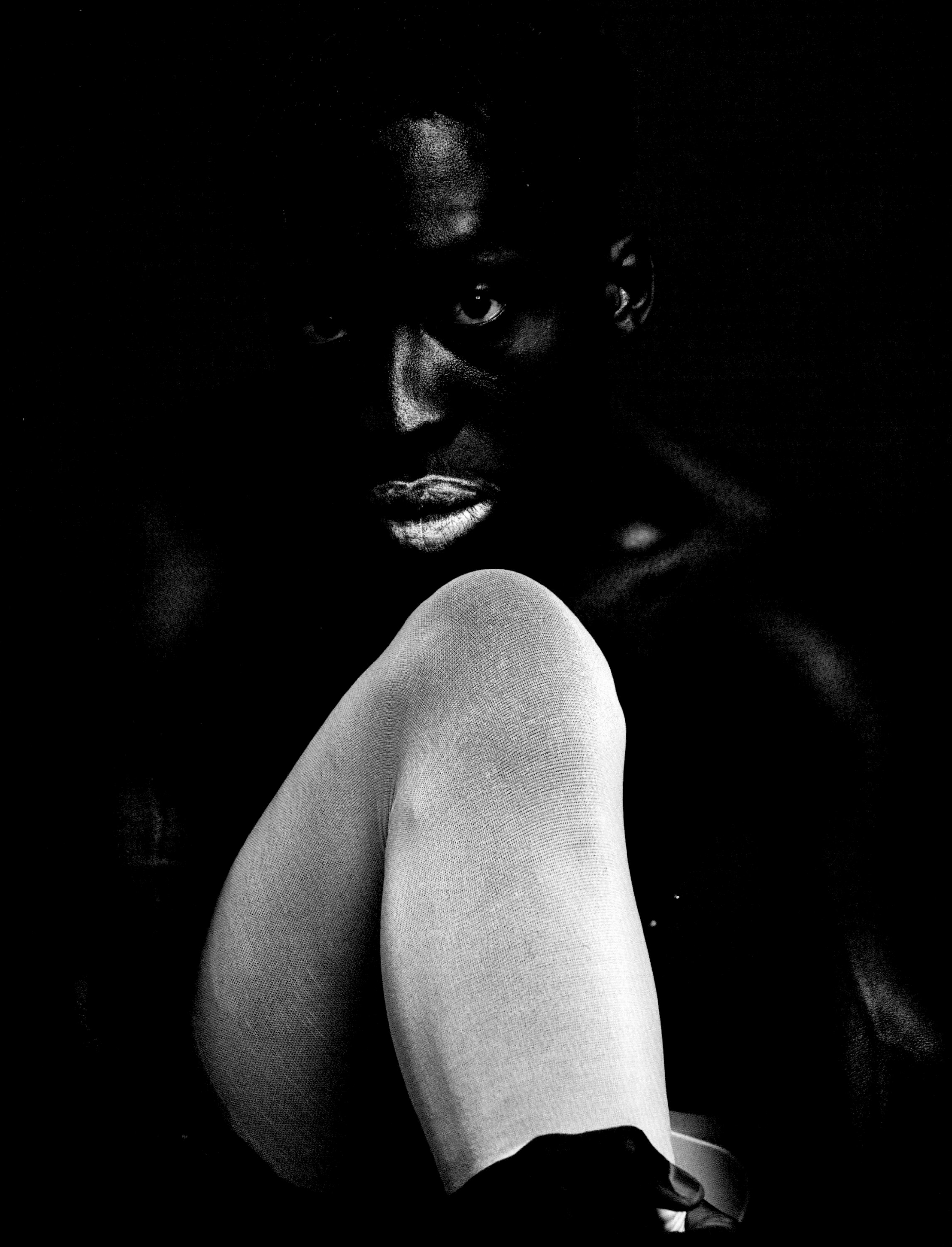

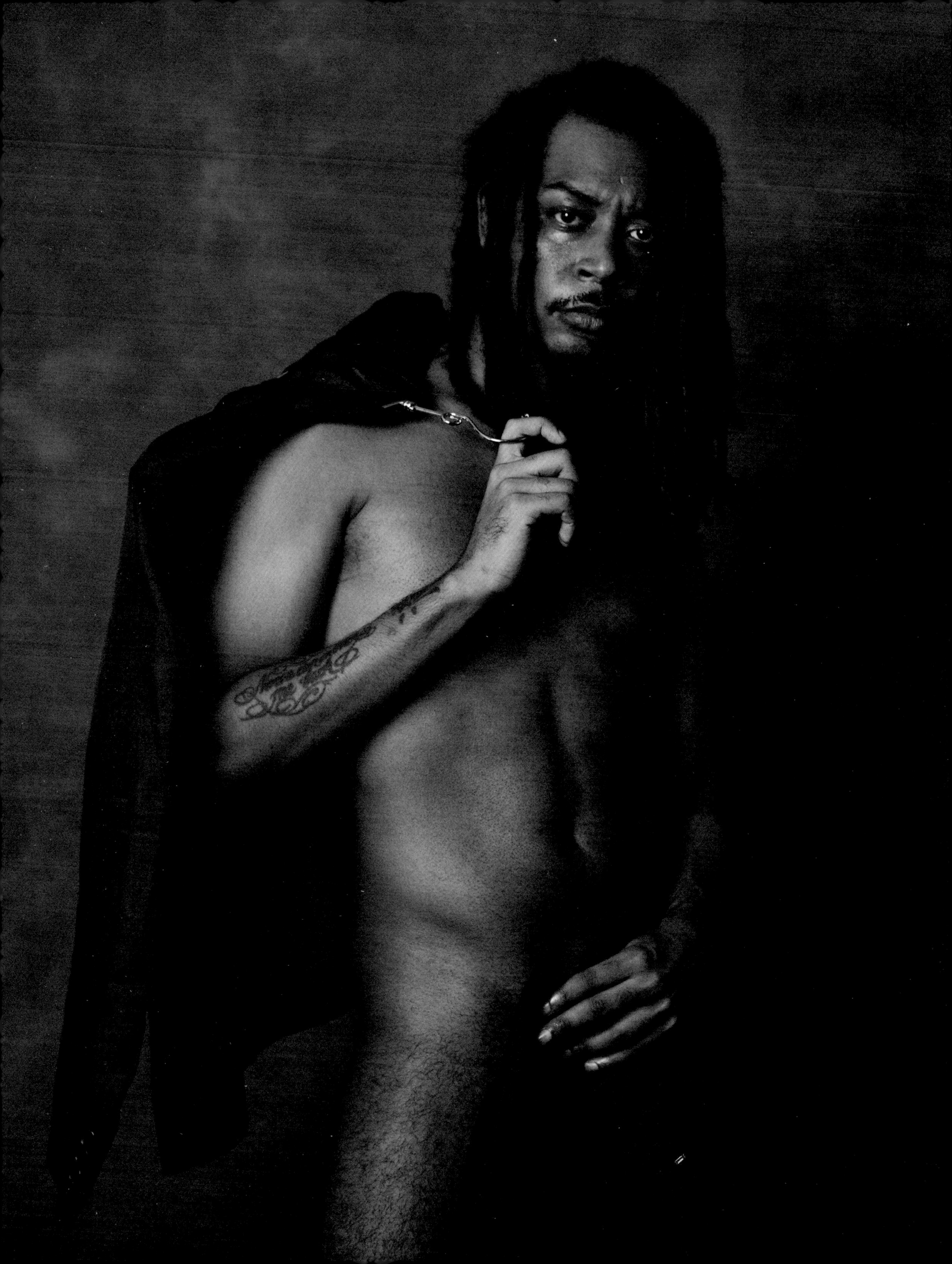

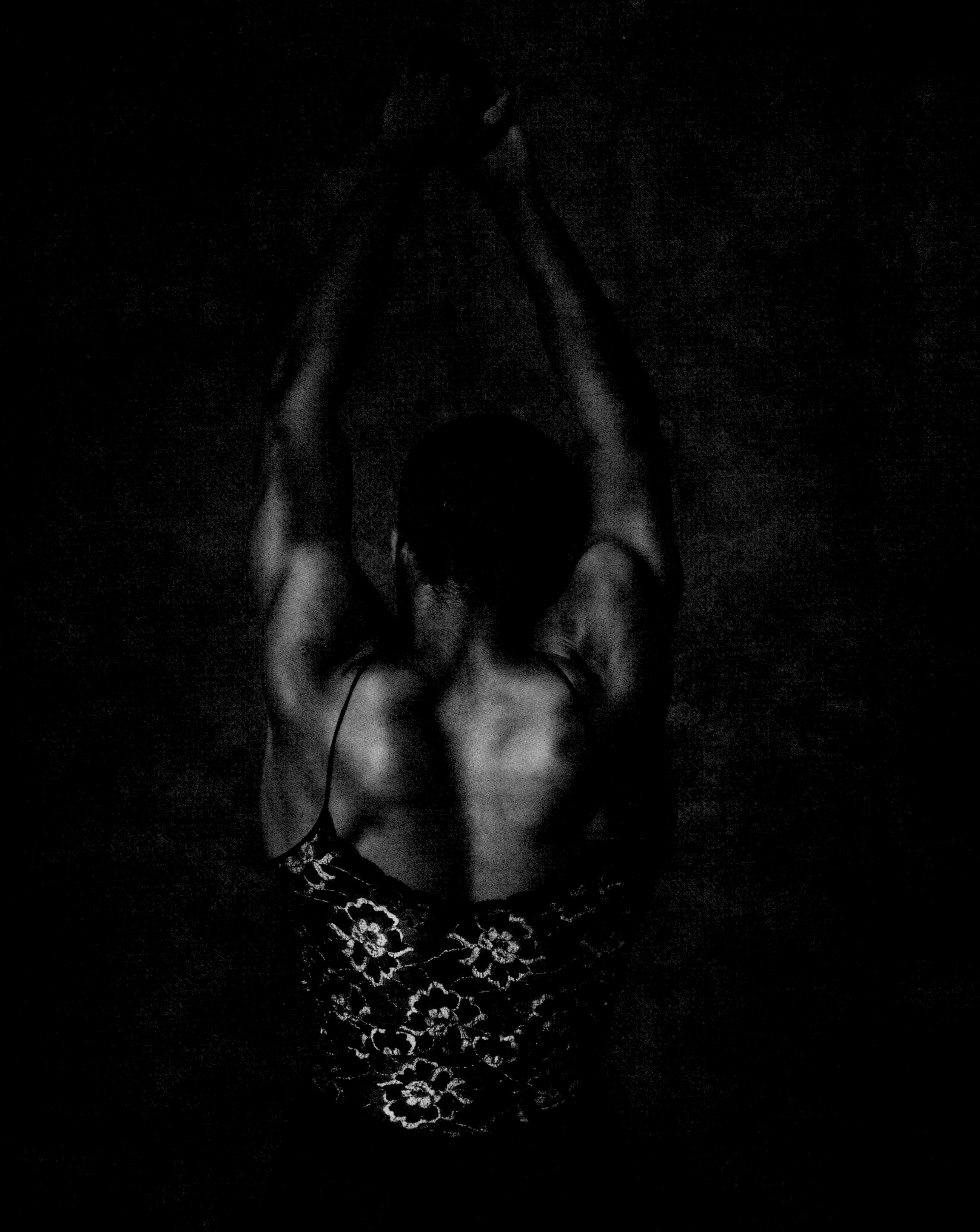

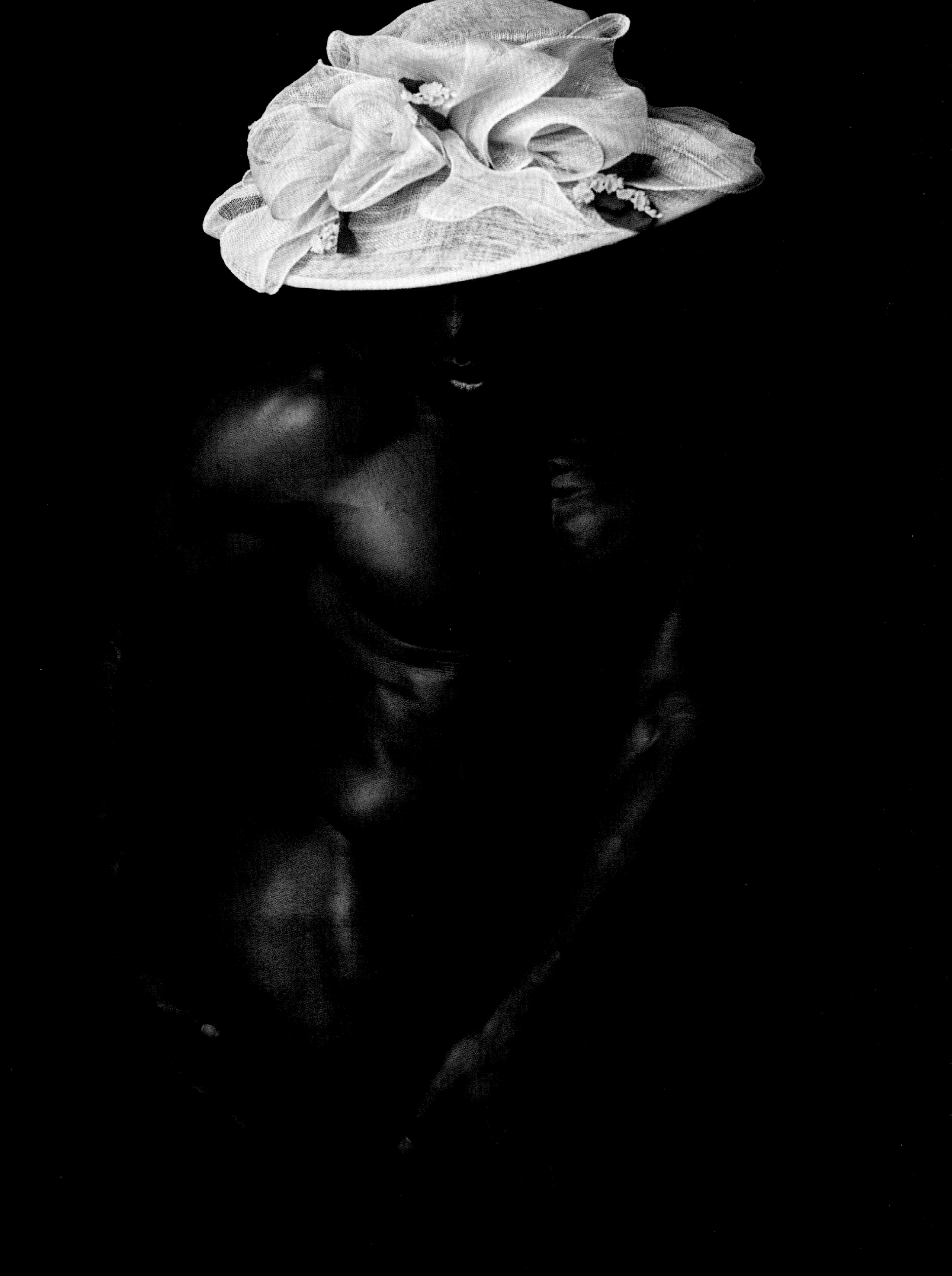

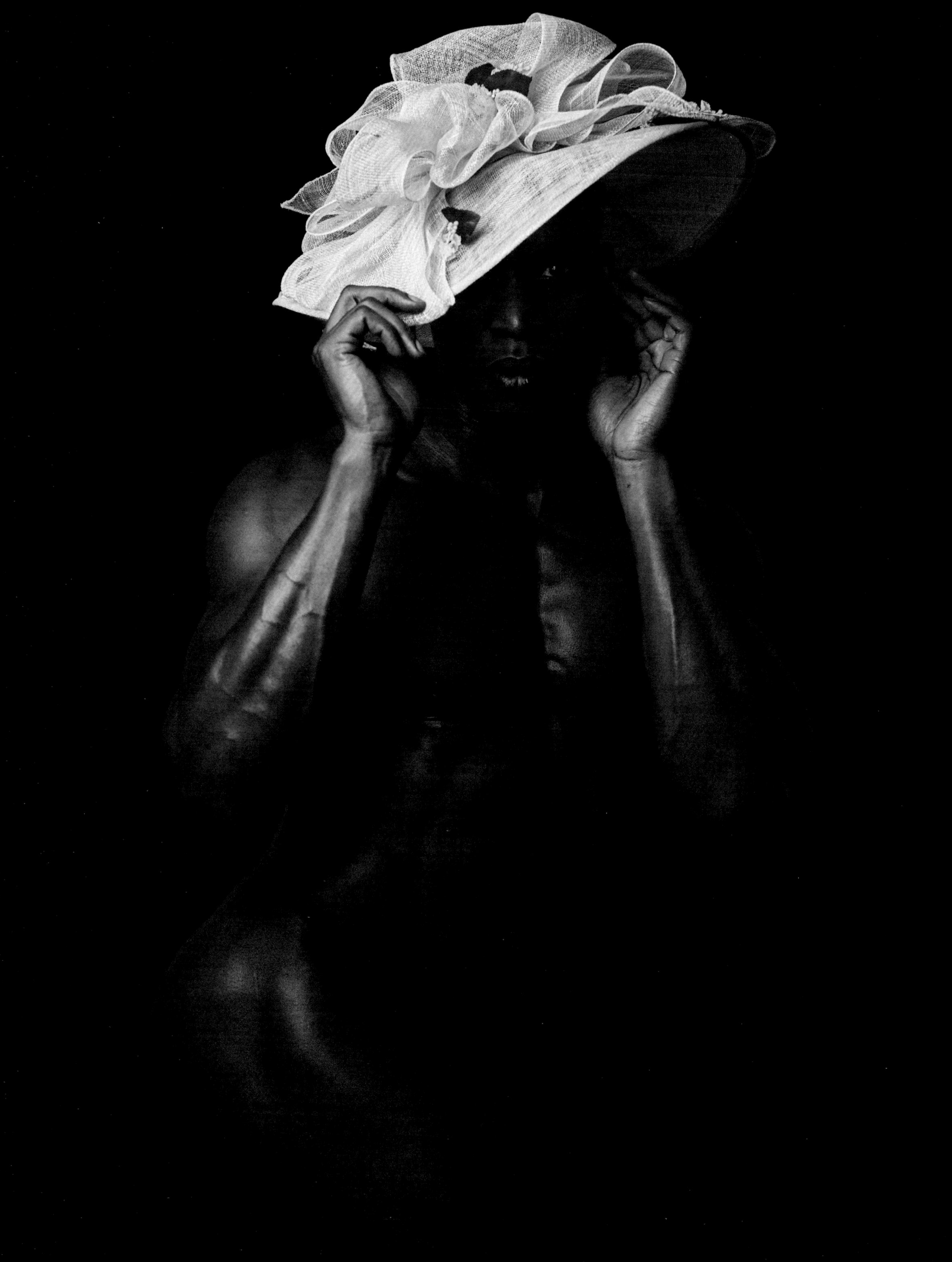

"CHILDREN HAVE NEVER BEEN VERY GOOD AT LISTENING TO THEIR ELDERS, BUT THEY HAVE NEVER FAILED TO IMITATE THEM"

- JAMES BALDWIN

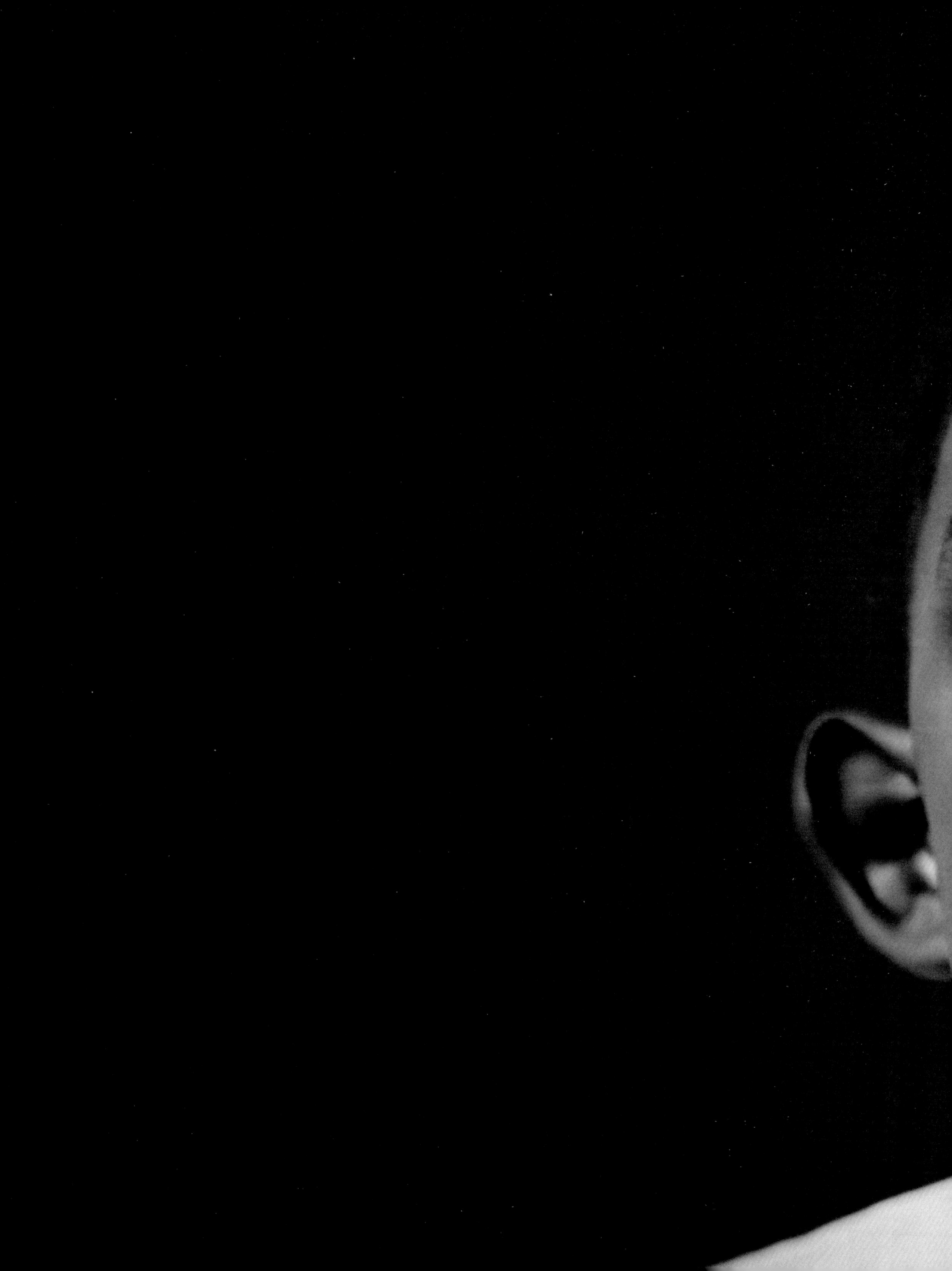

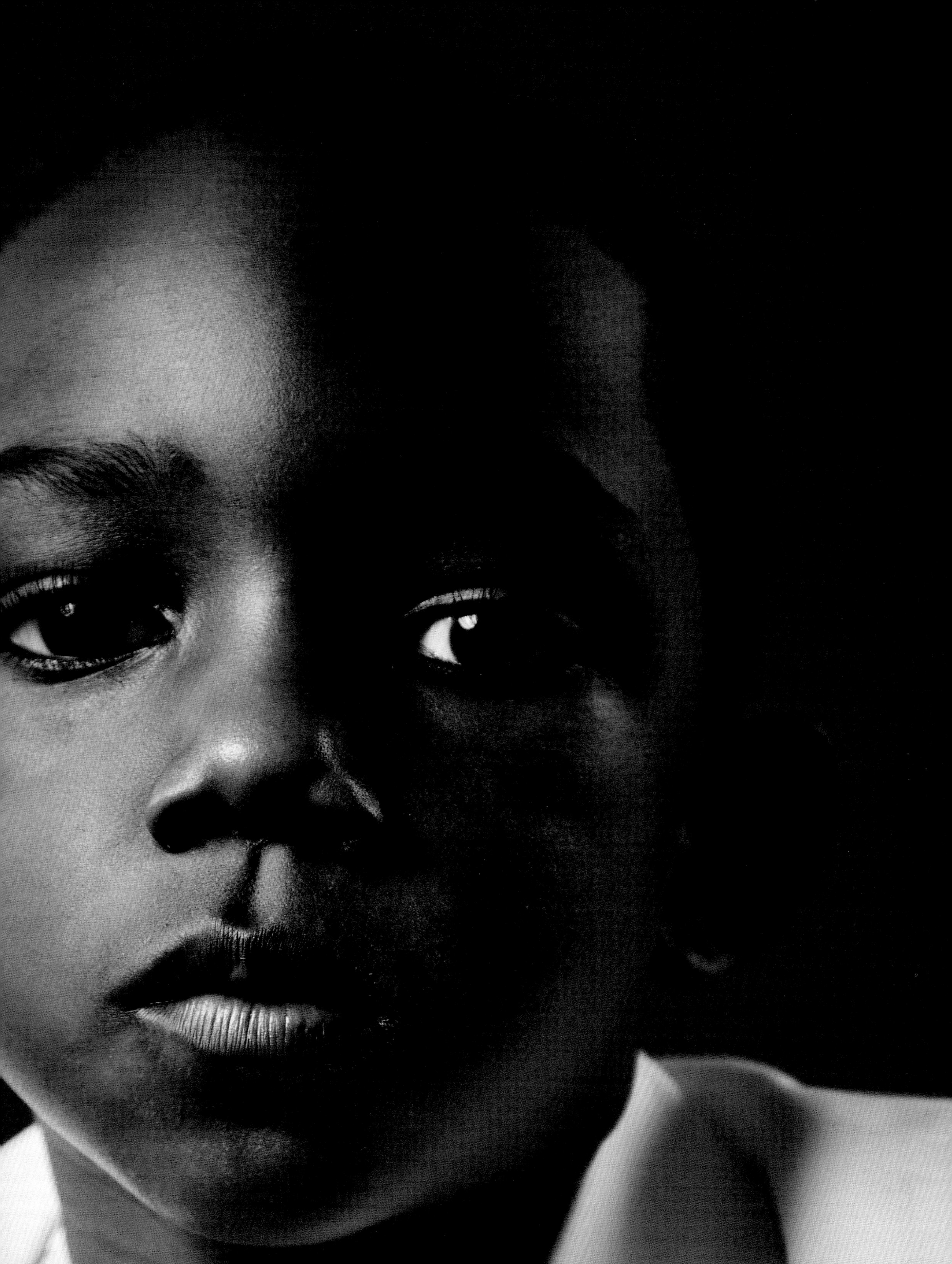

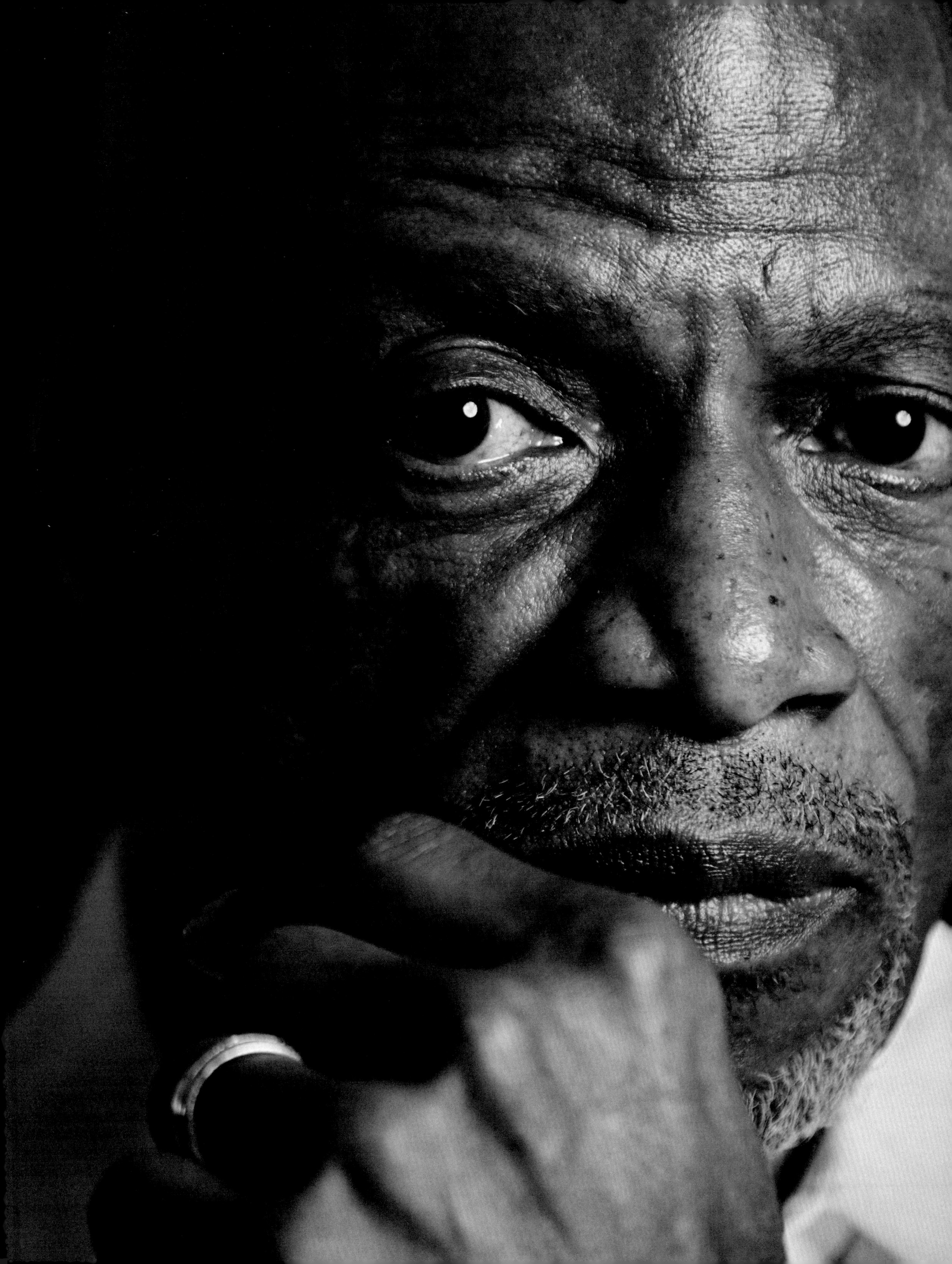

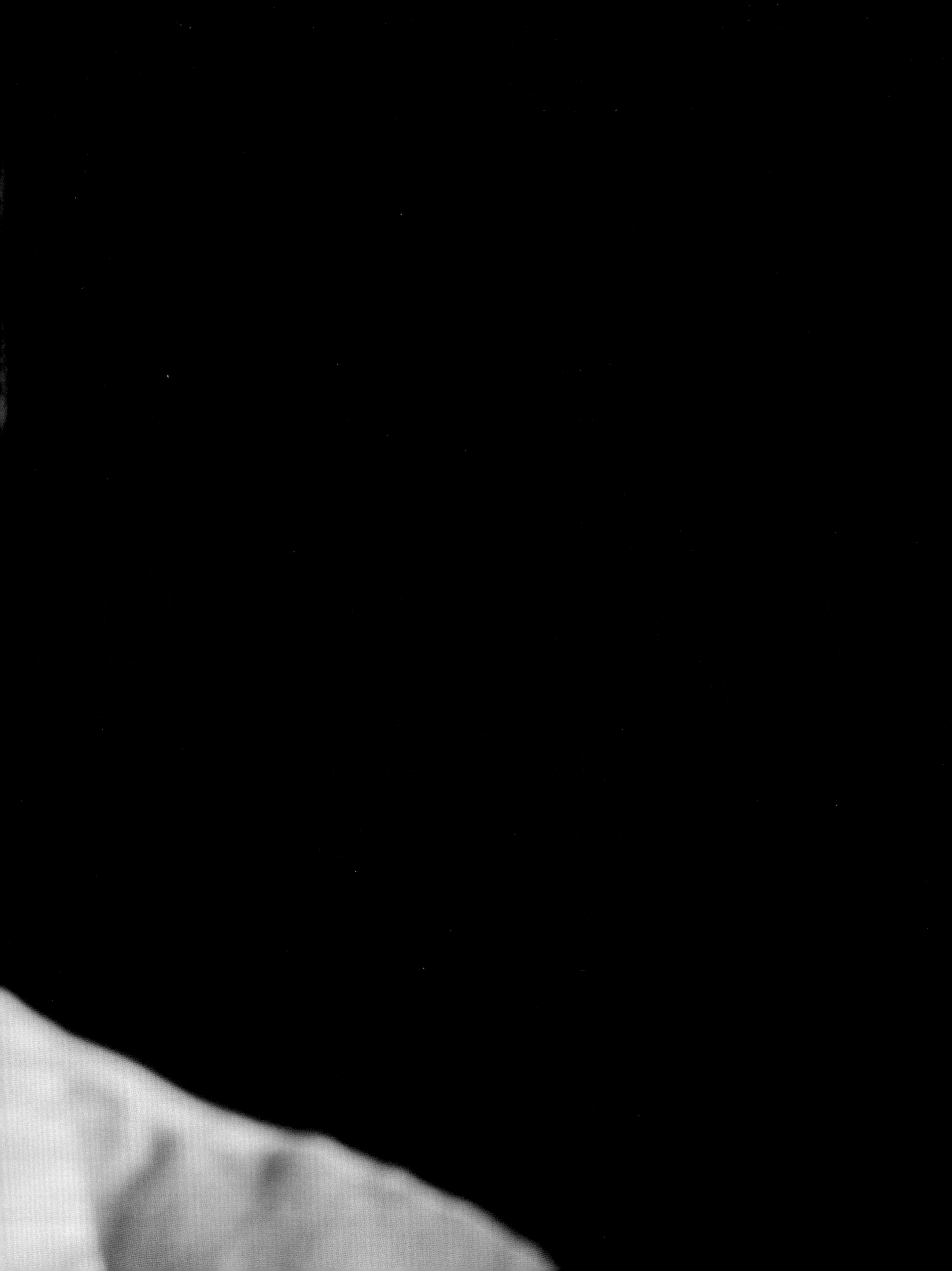

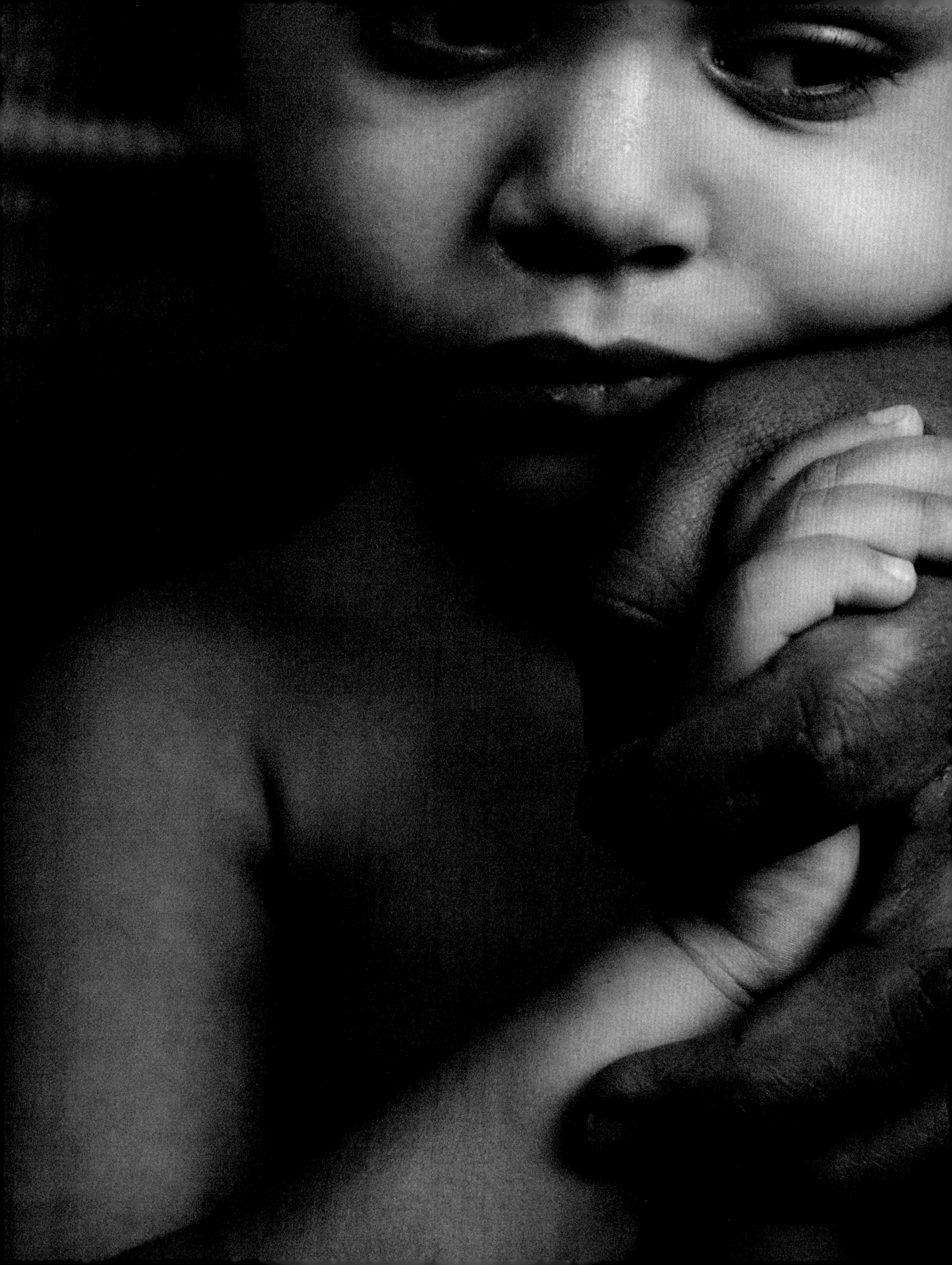

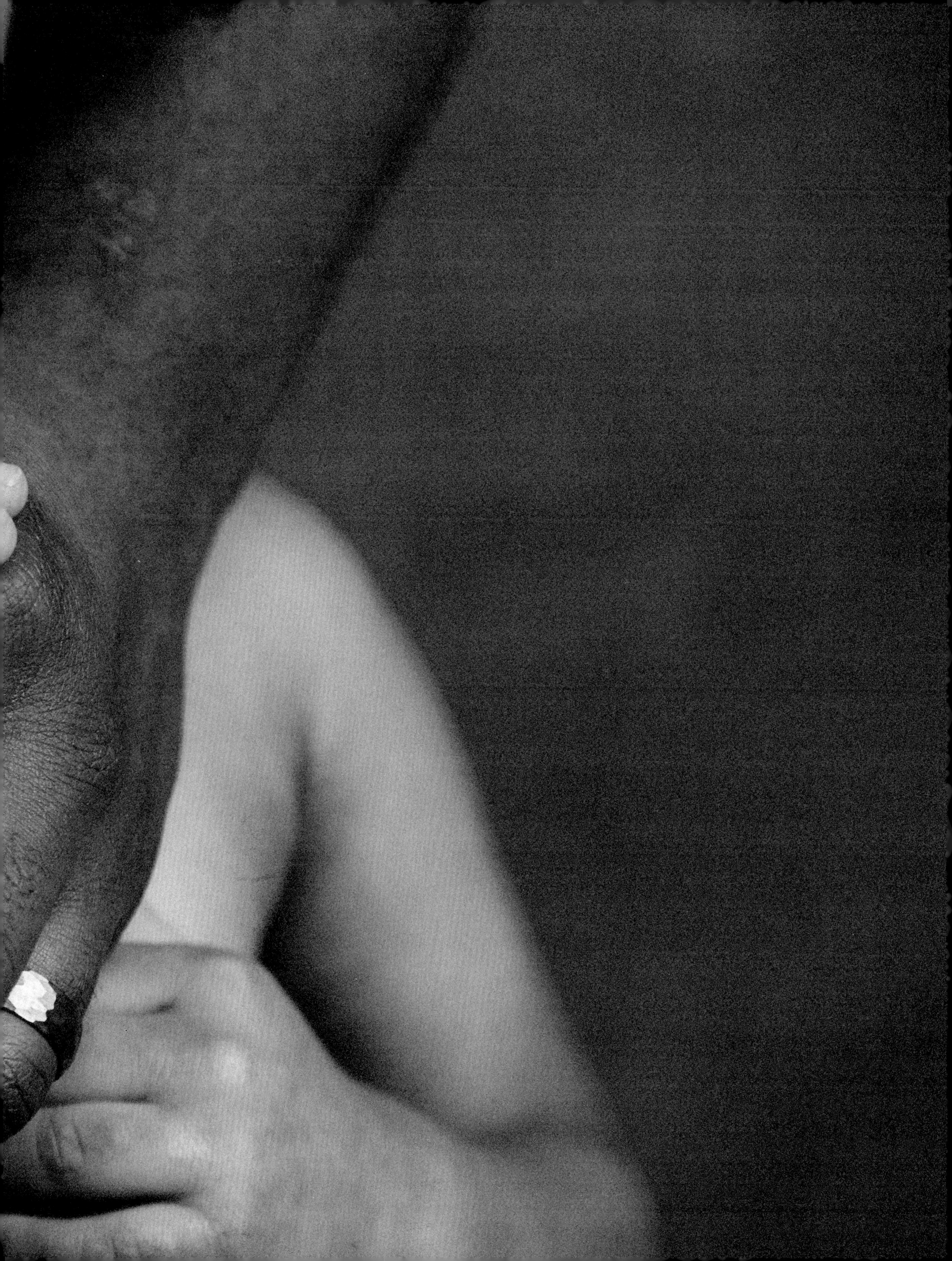

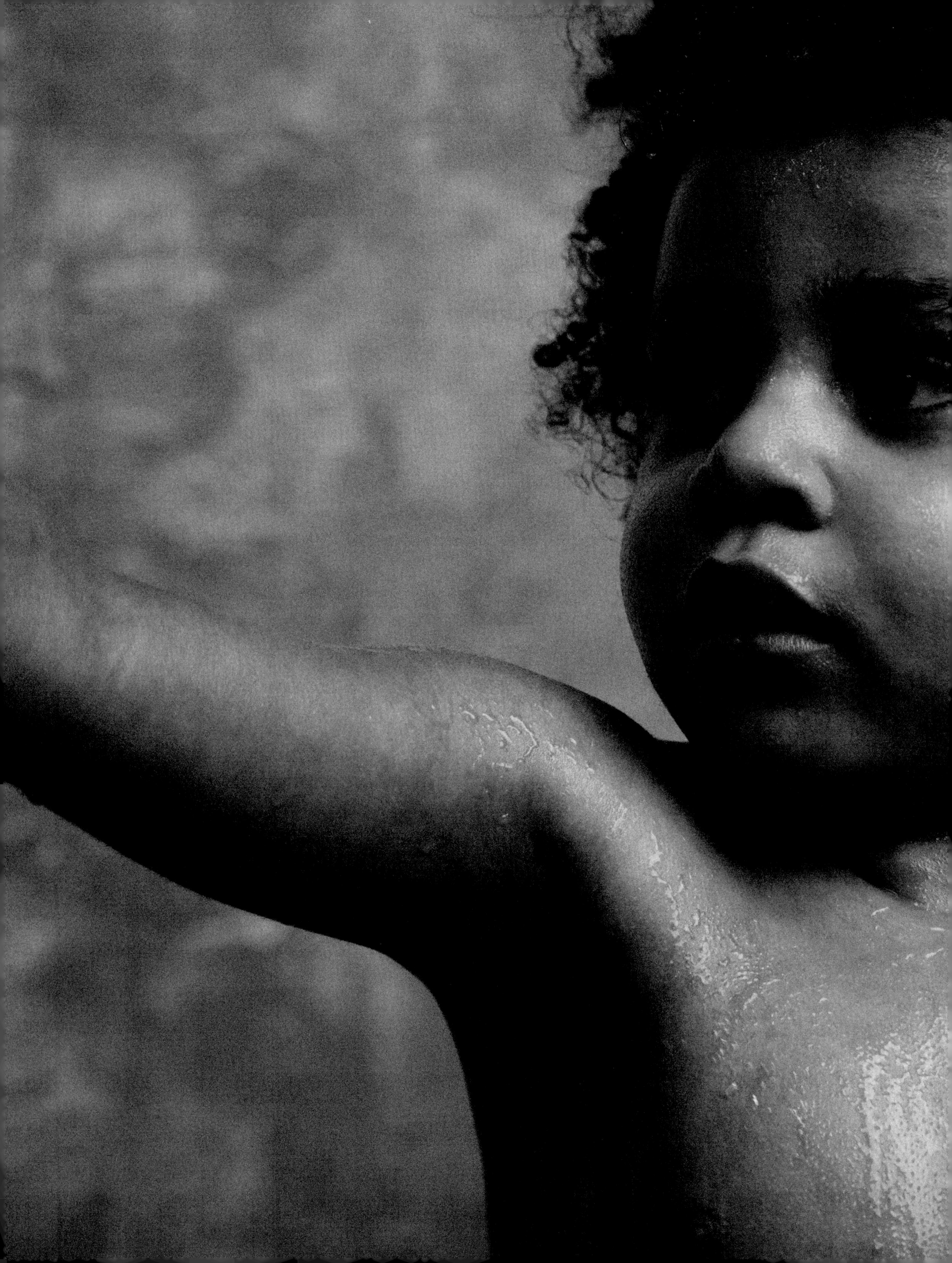

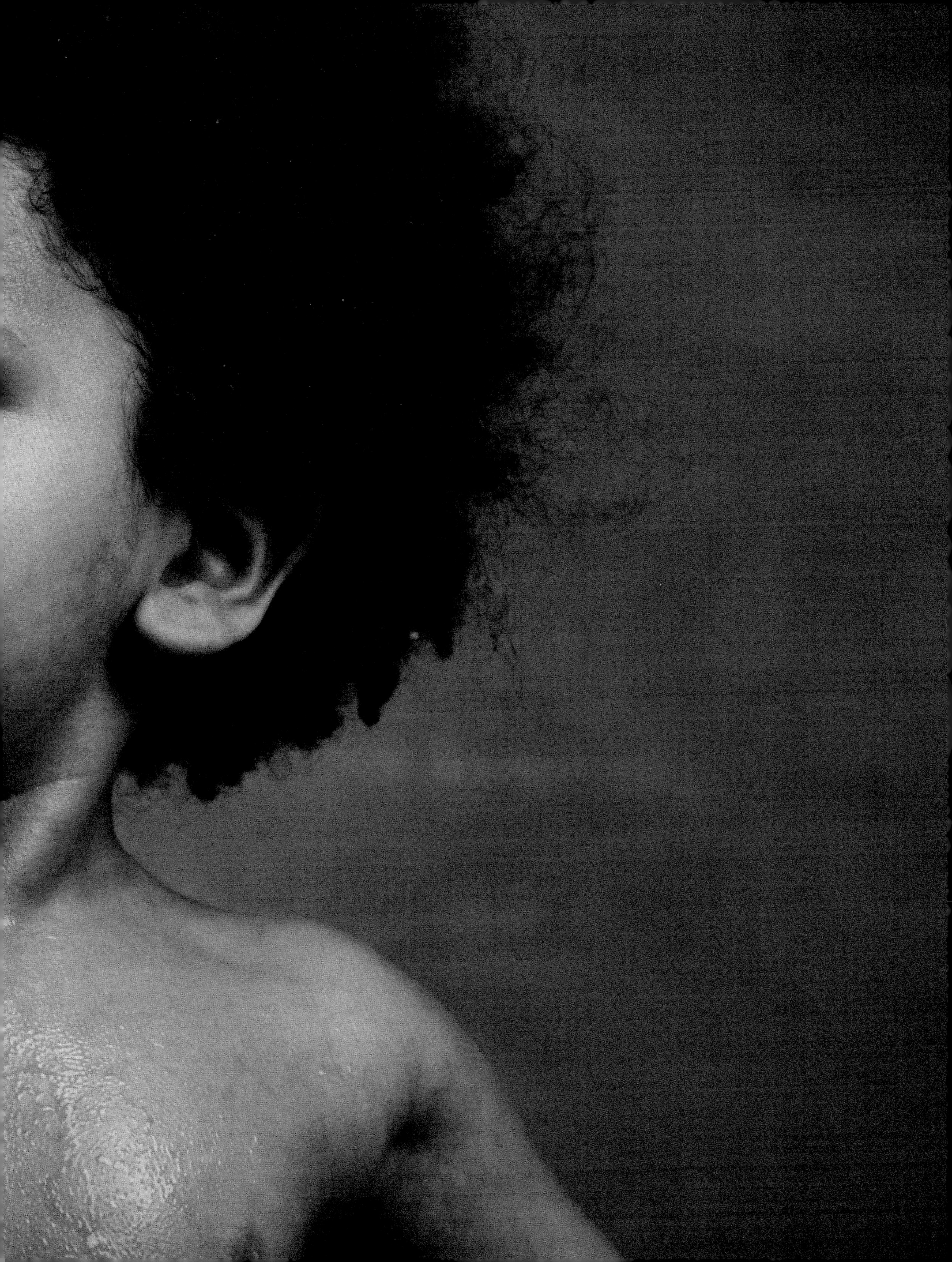

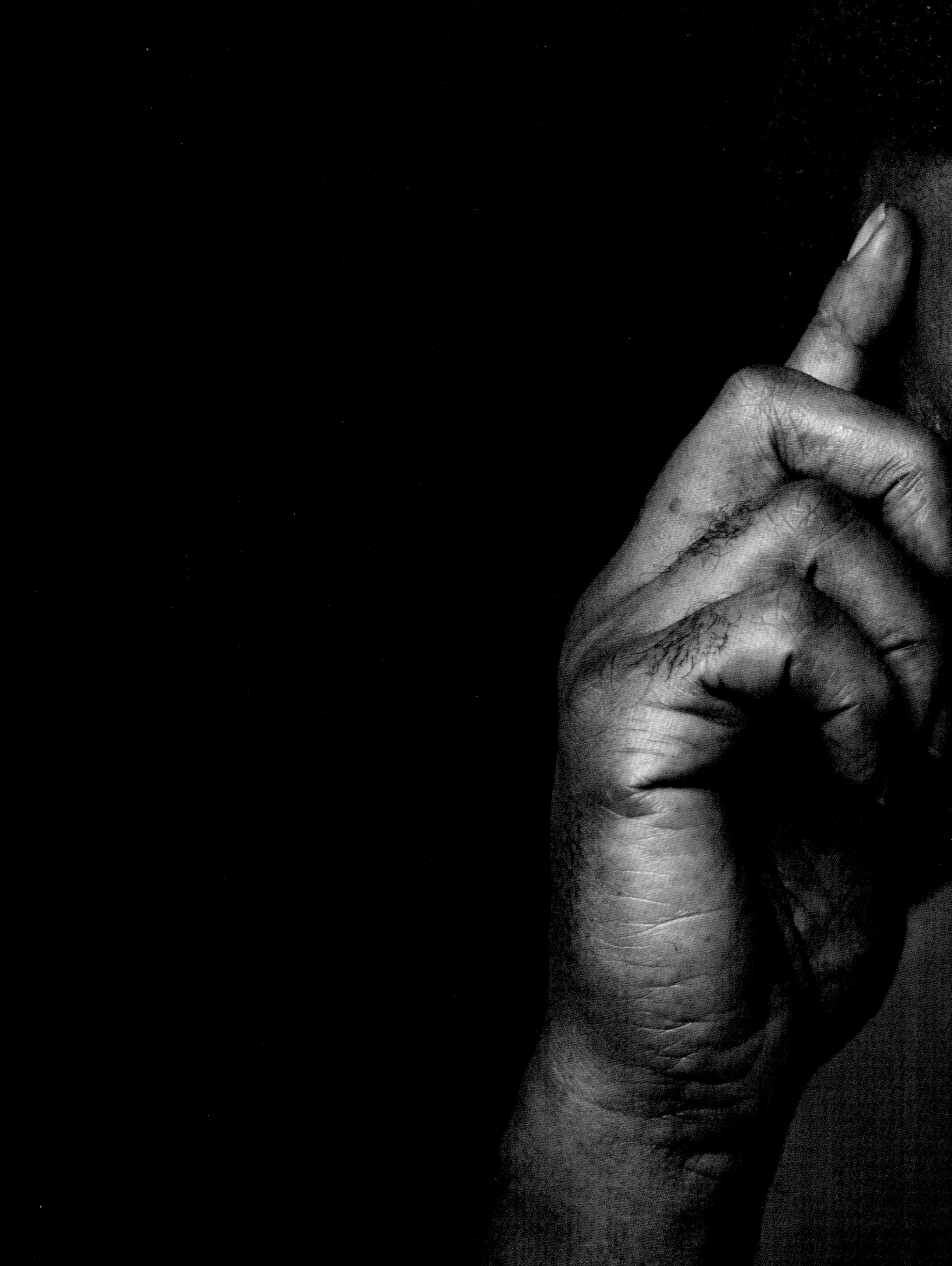

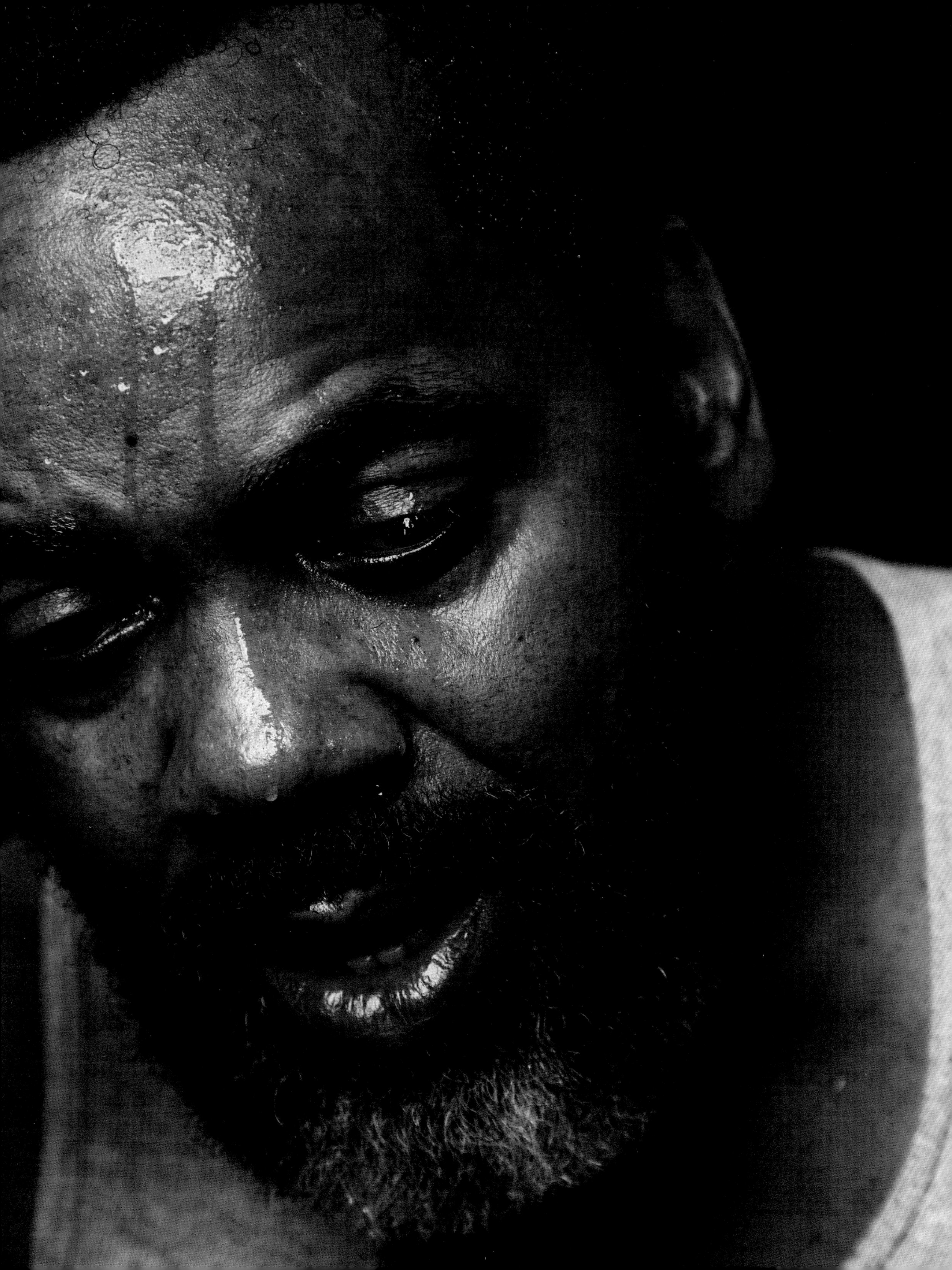

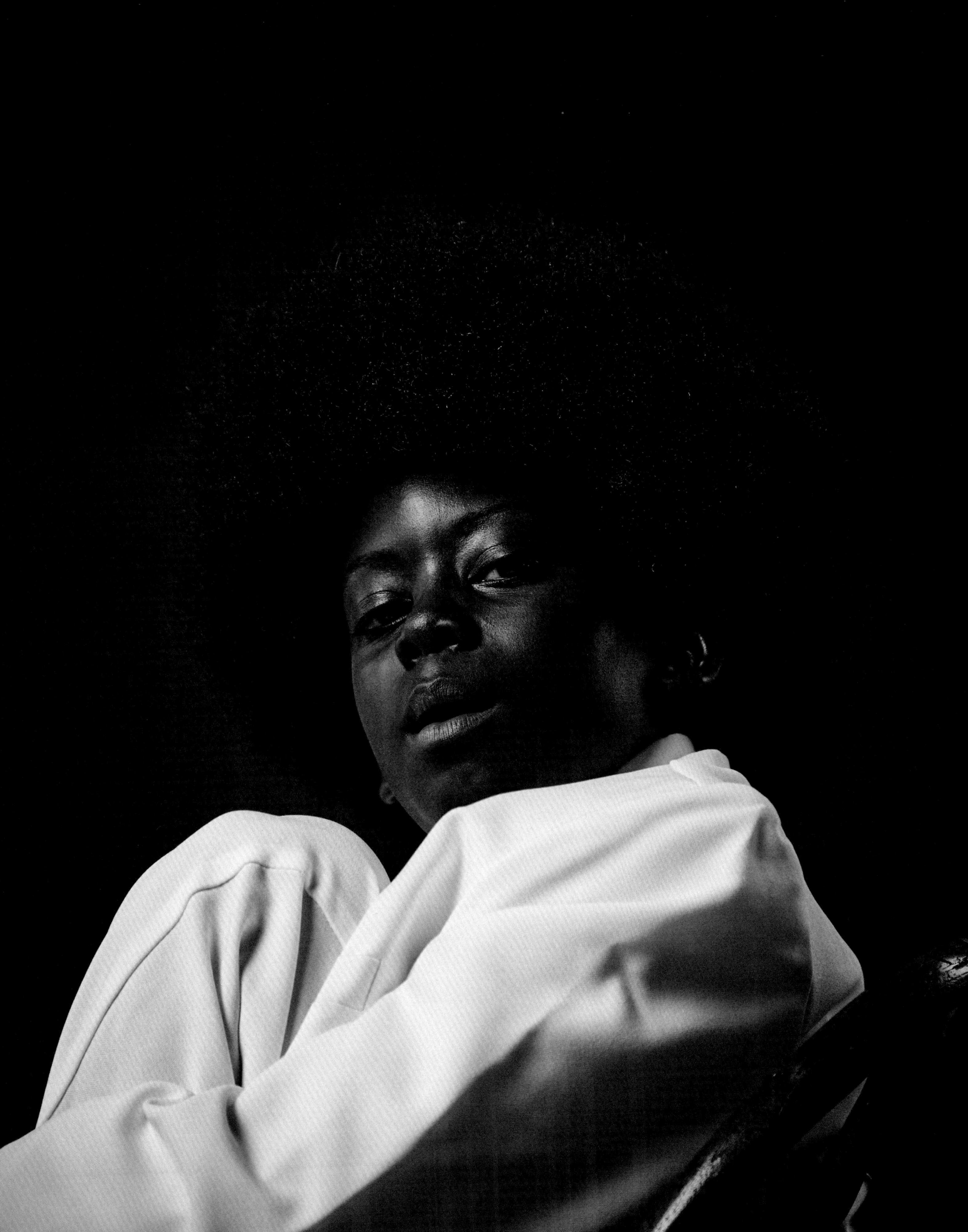

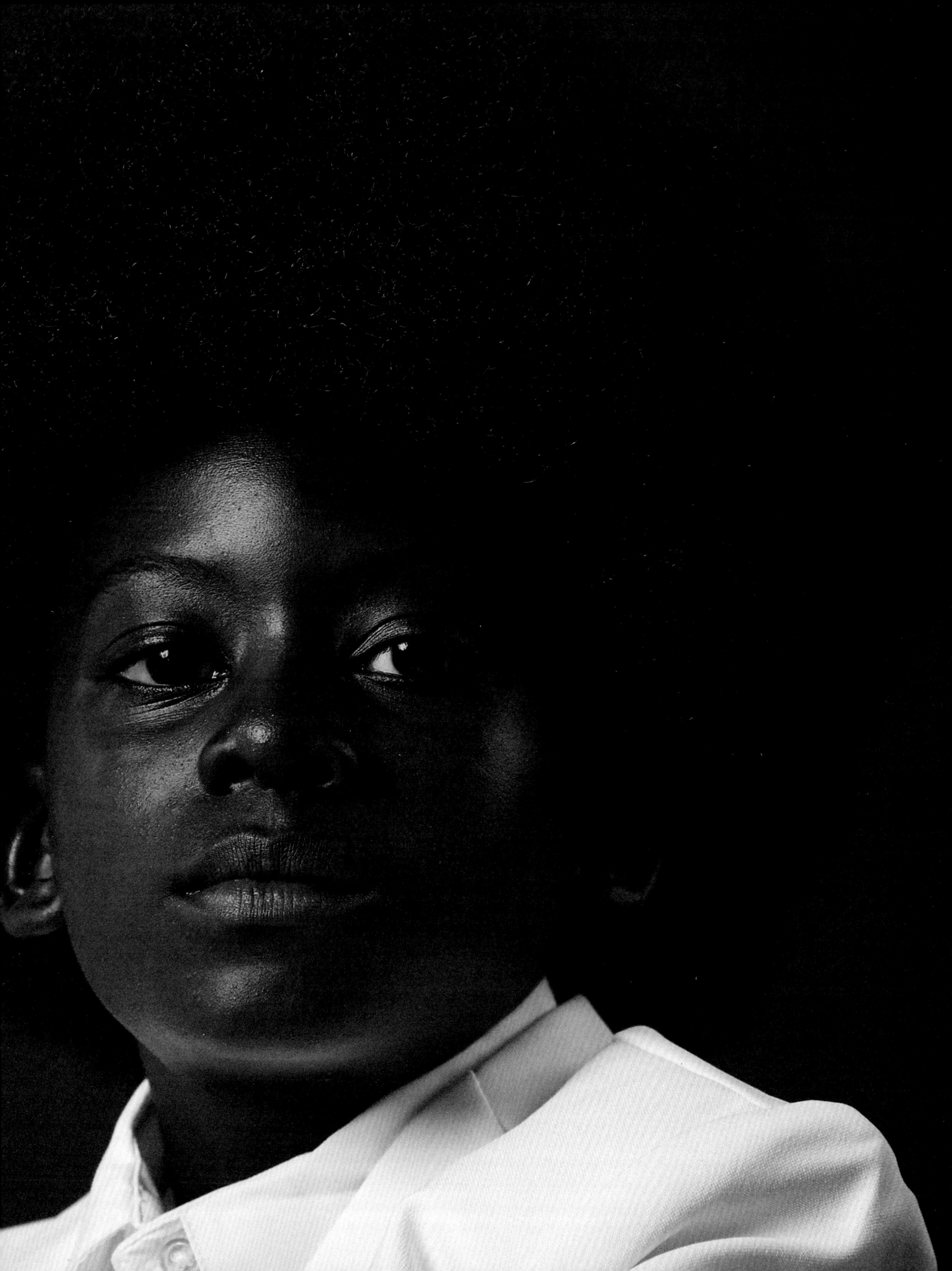

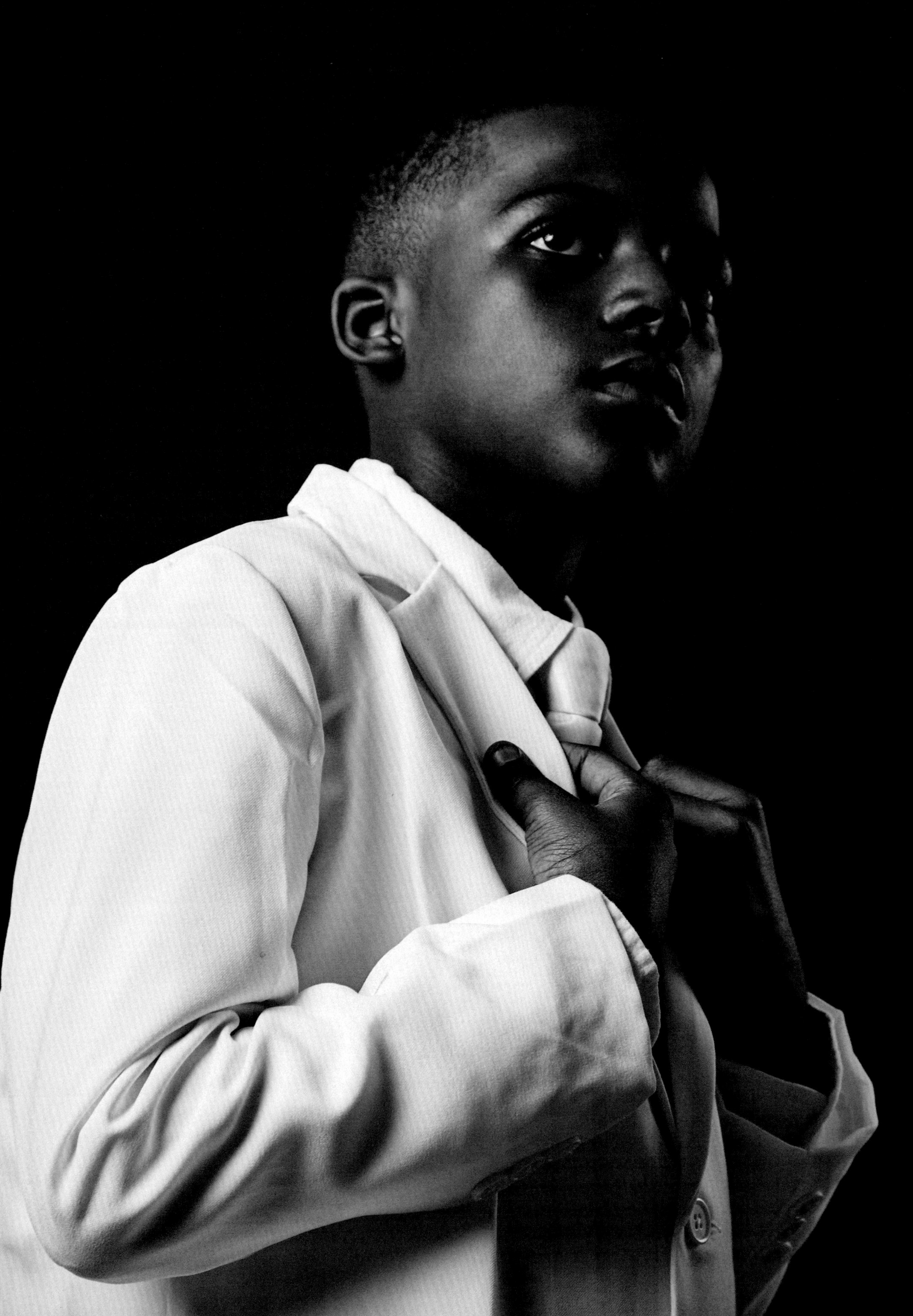

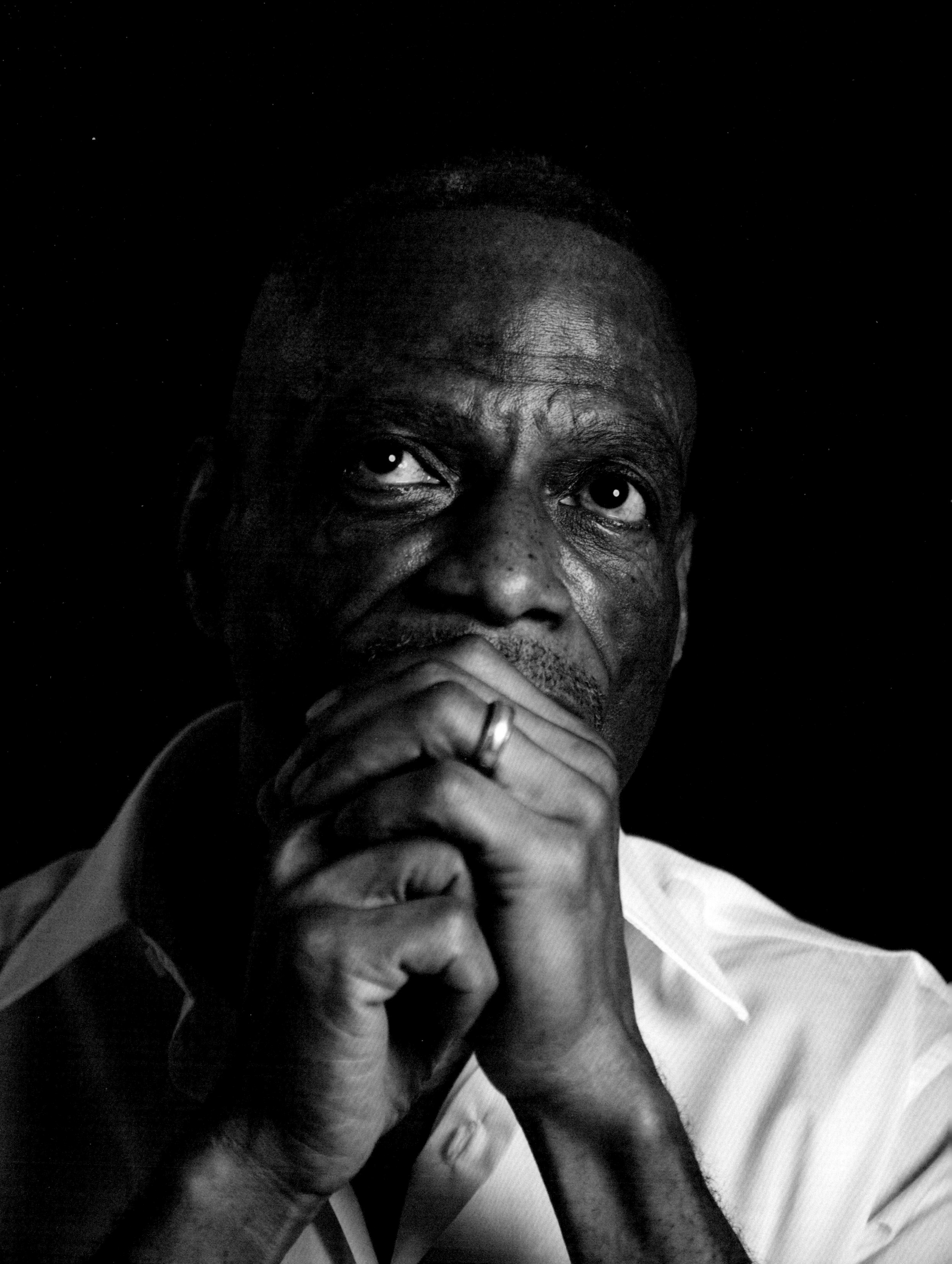

“ONE OF THE PROCESSES OF YOUR LIFE IS TO CONSTANTLY BREAK DOWN THAT INFERIORITY, TO CONSTANTLY REAFFIRM THAT I AM SOMEBODY”

- ALVIN AILEY

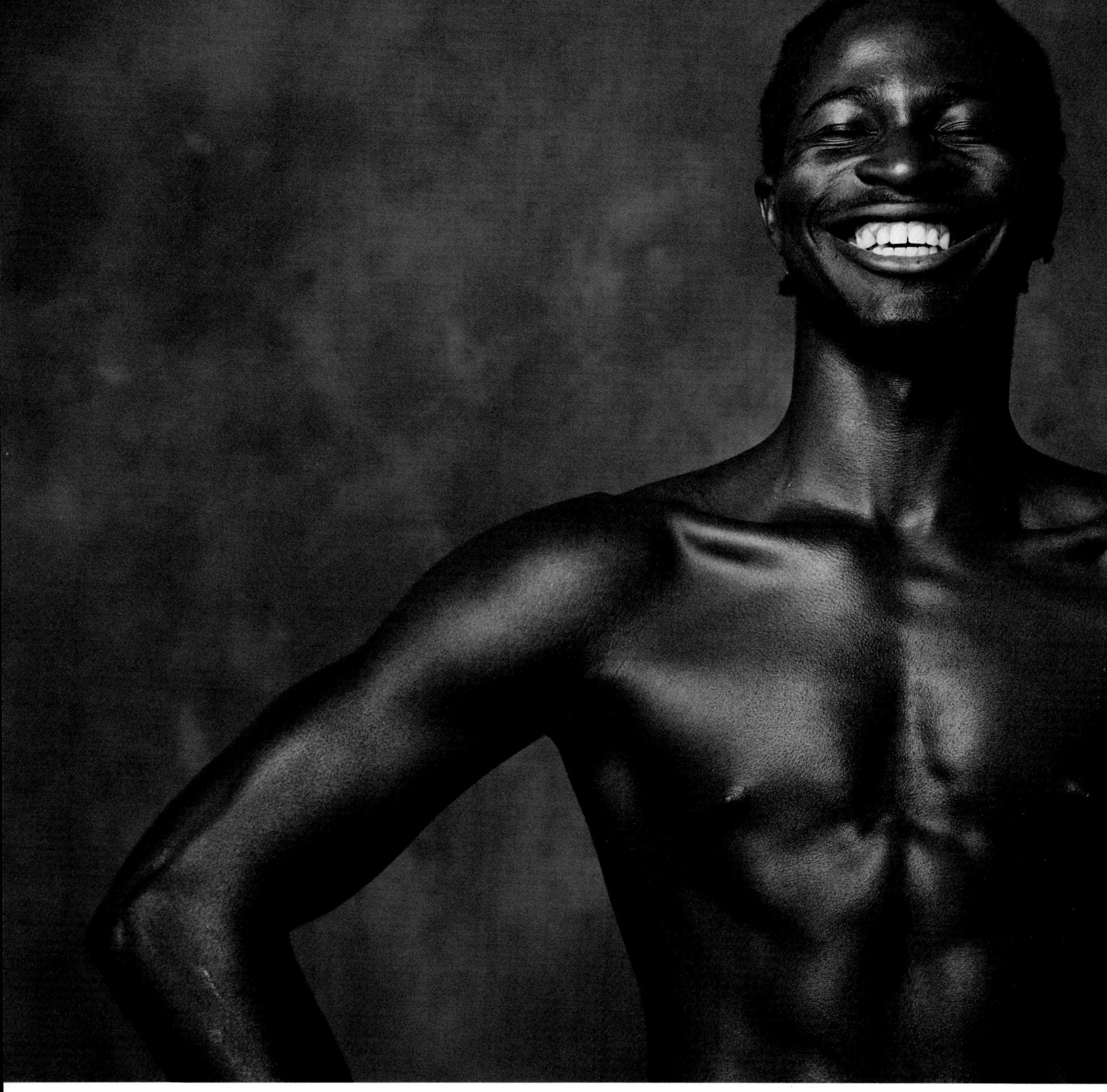

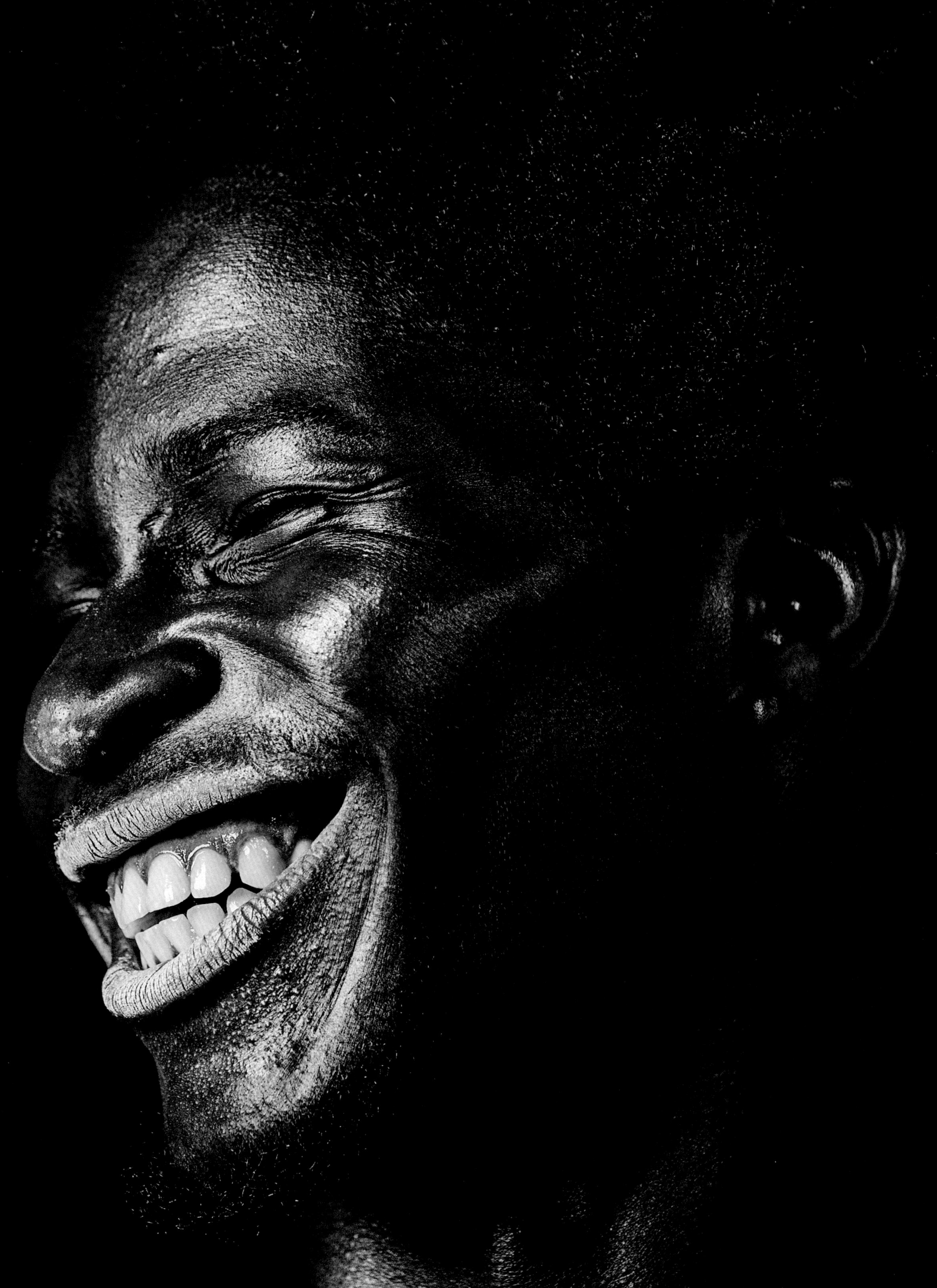

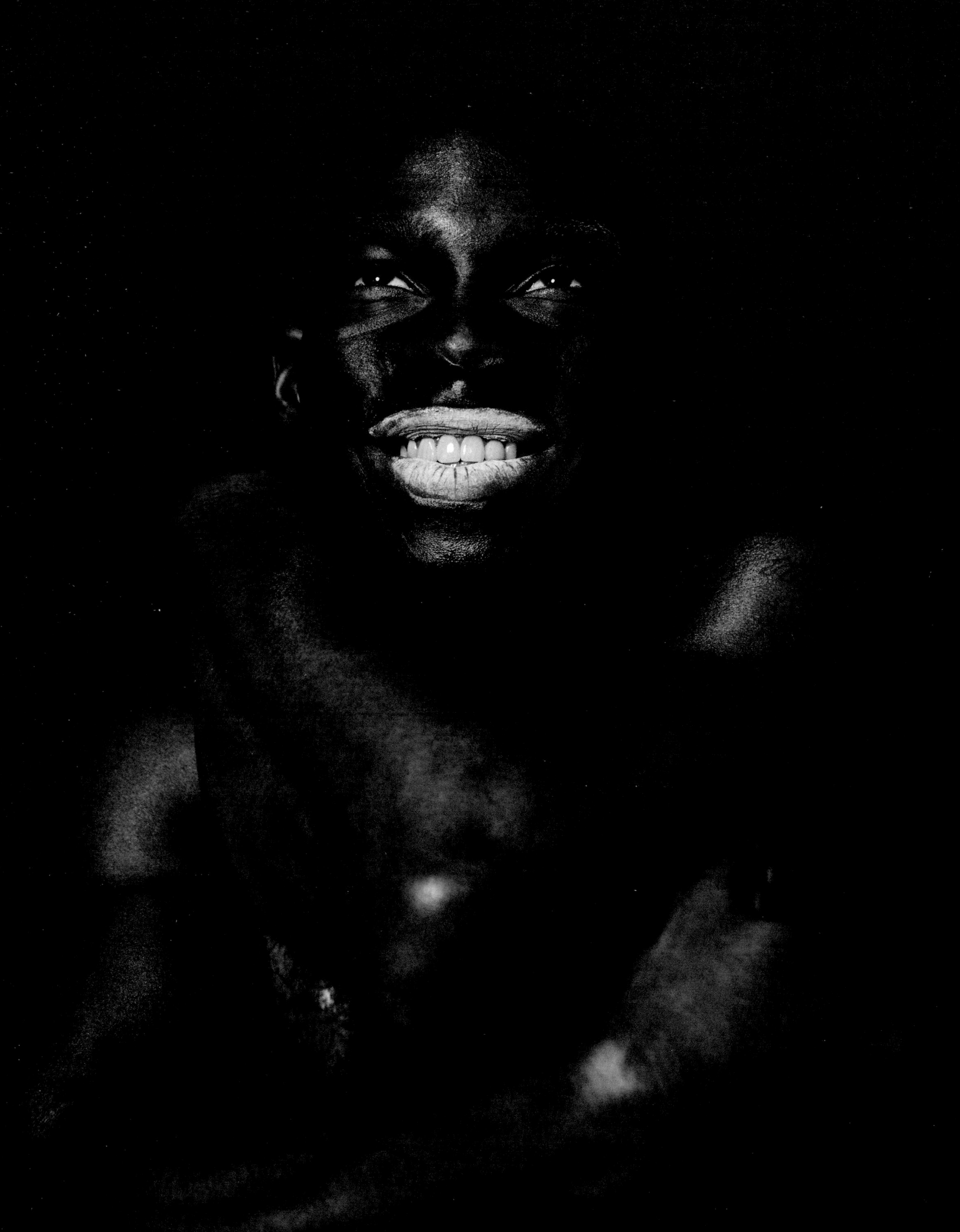

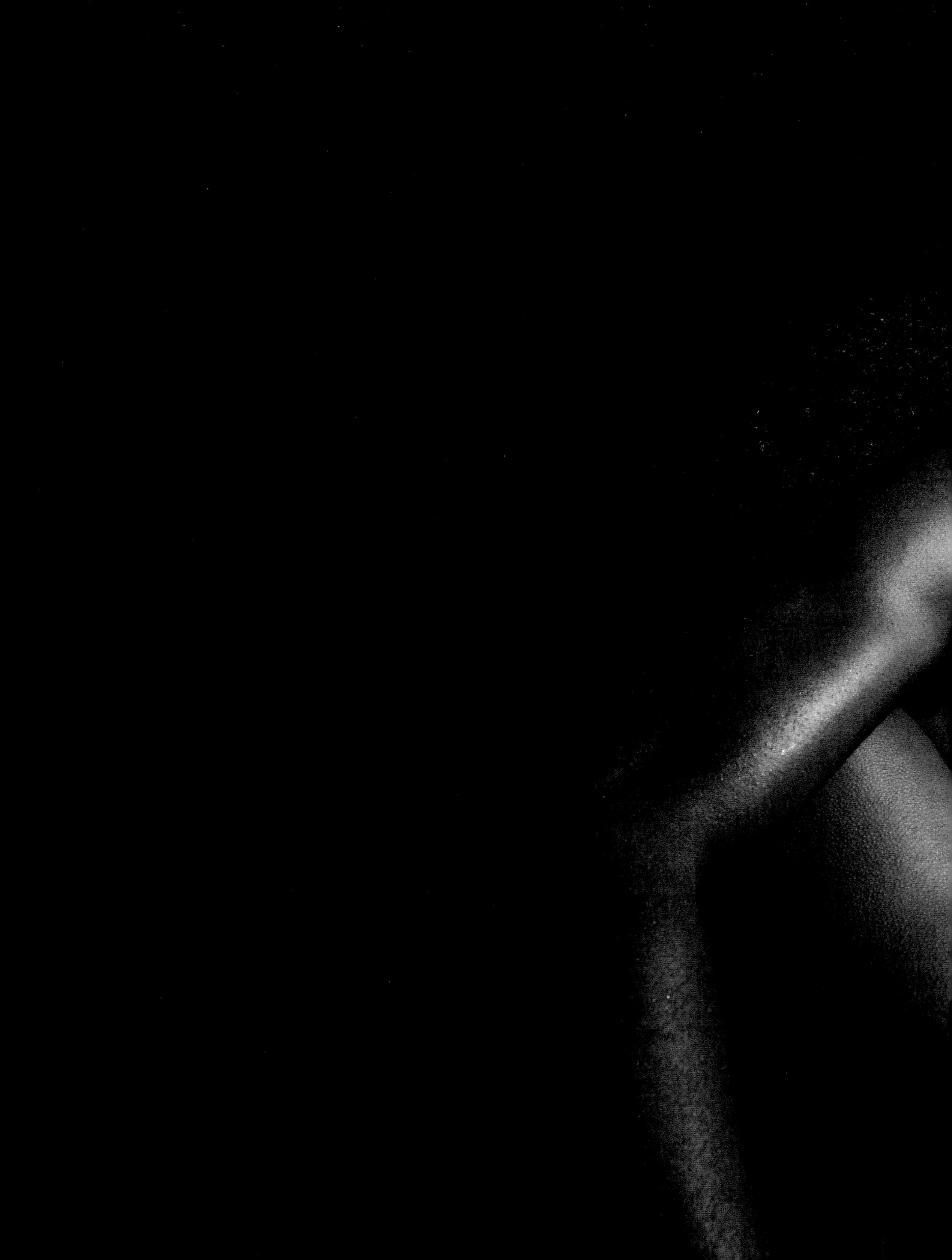

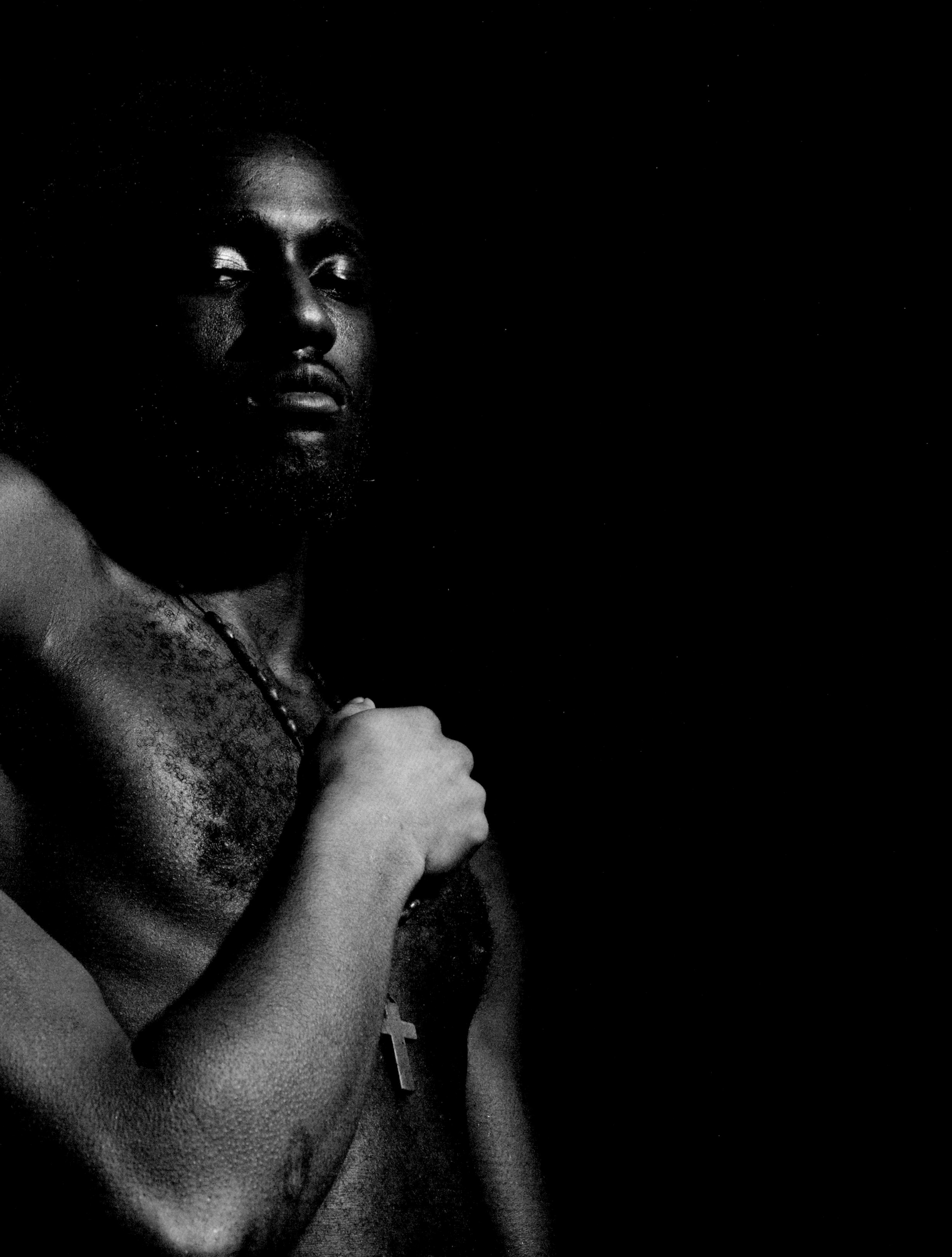

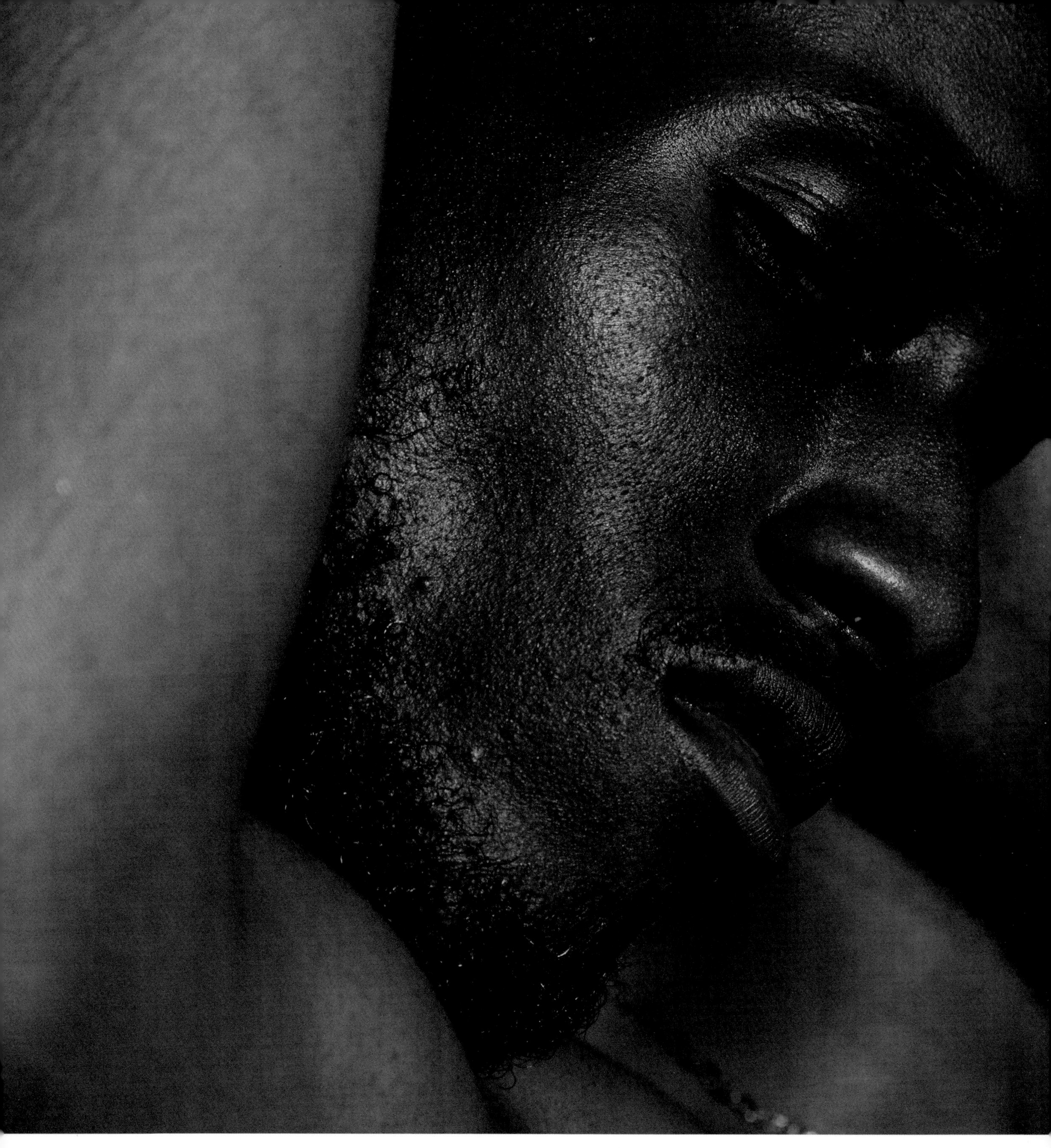

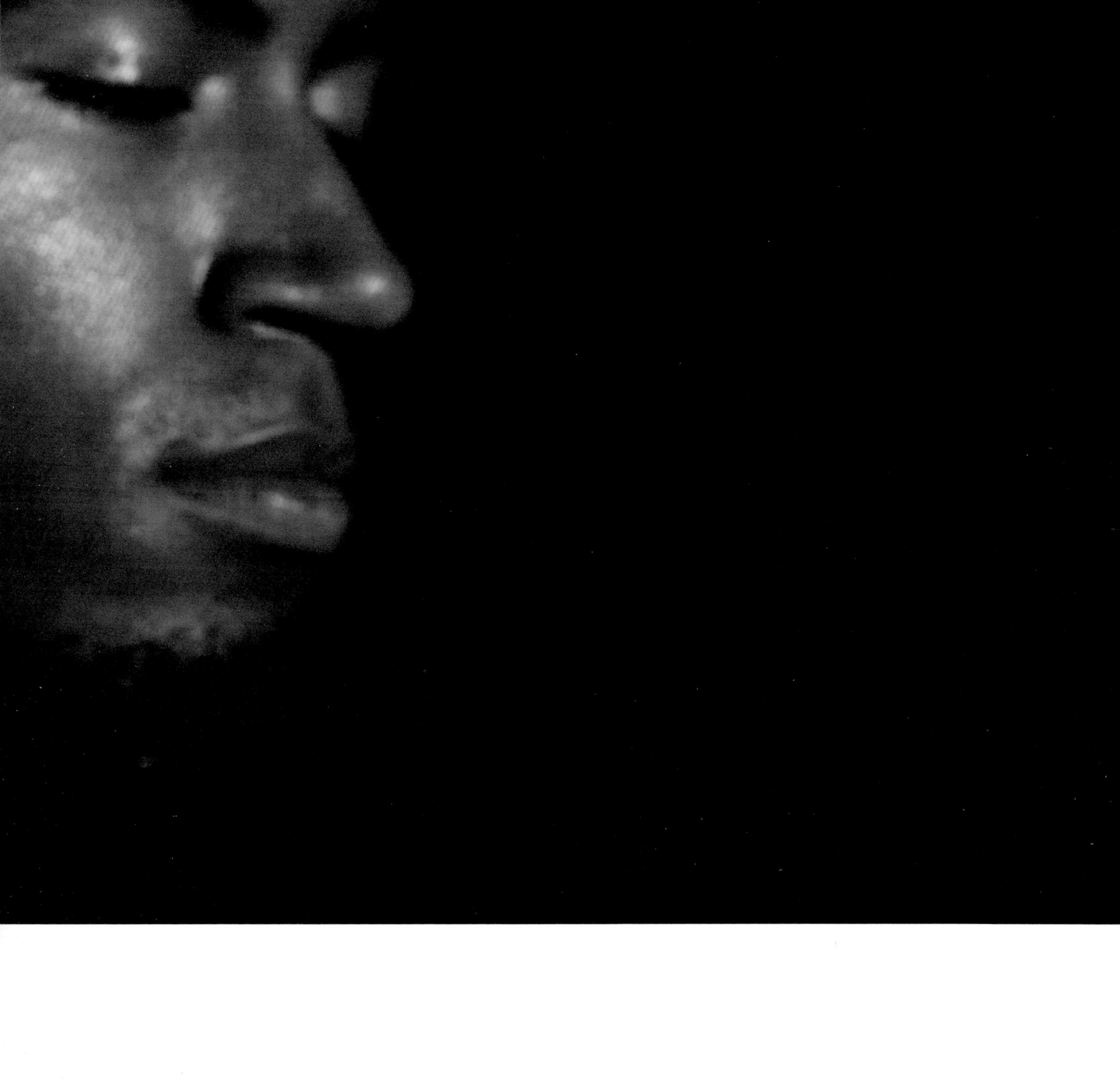

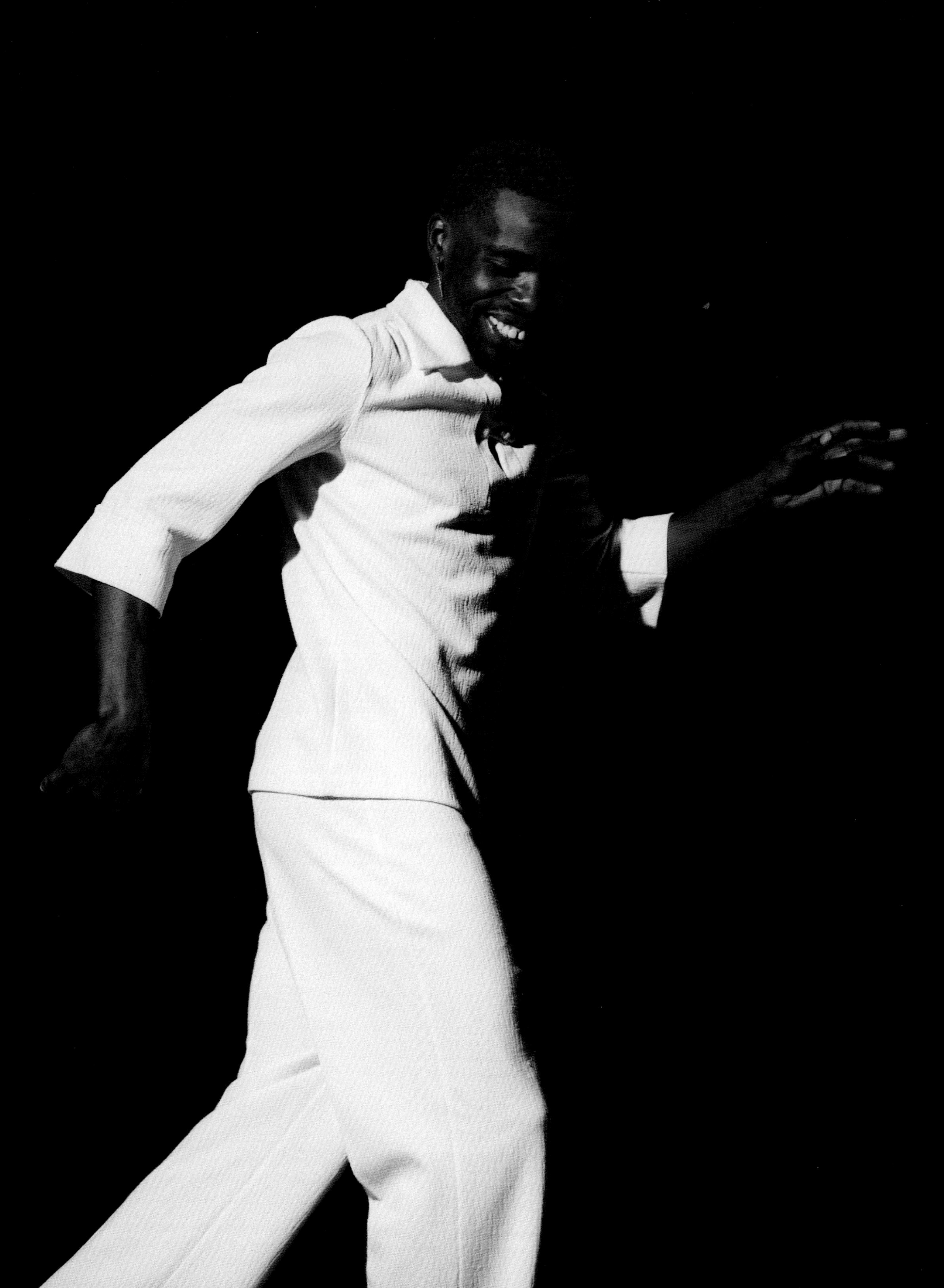

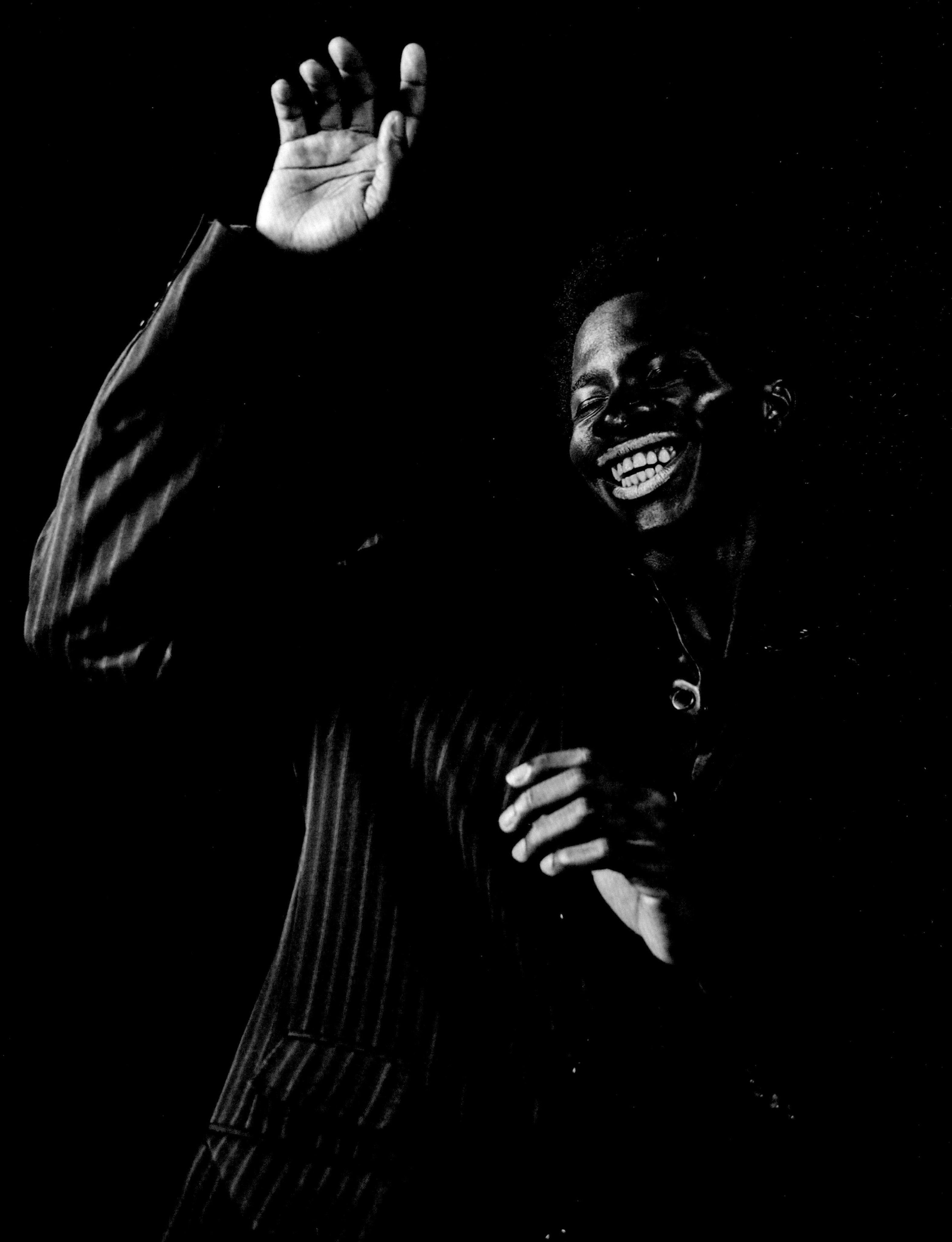

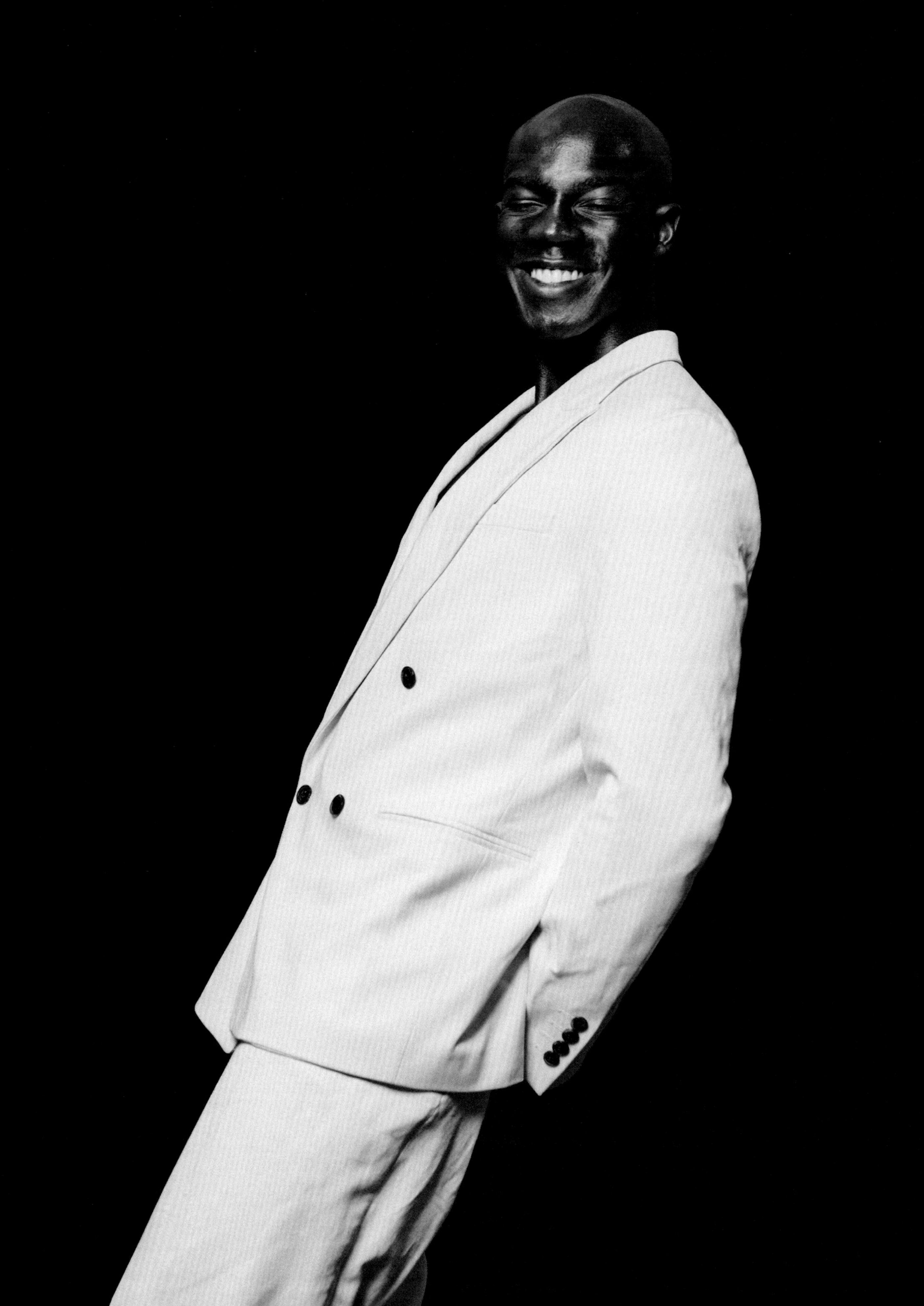

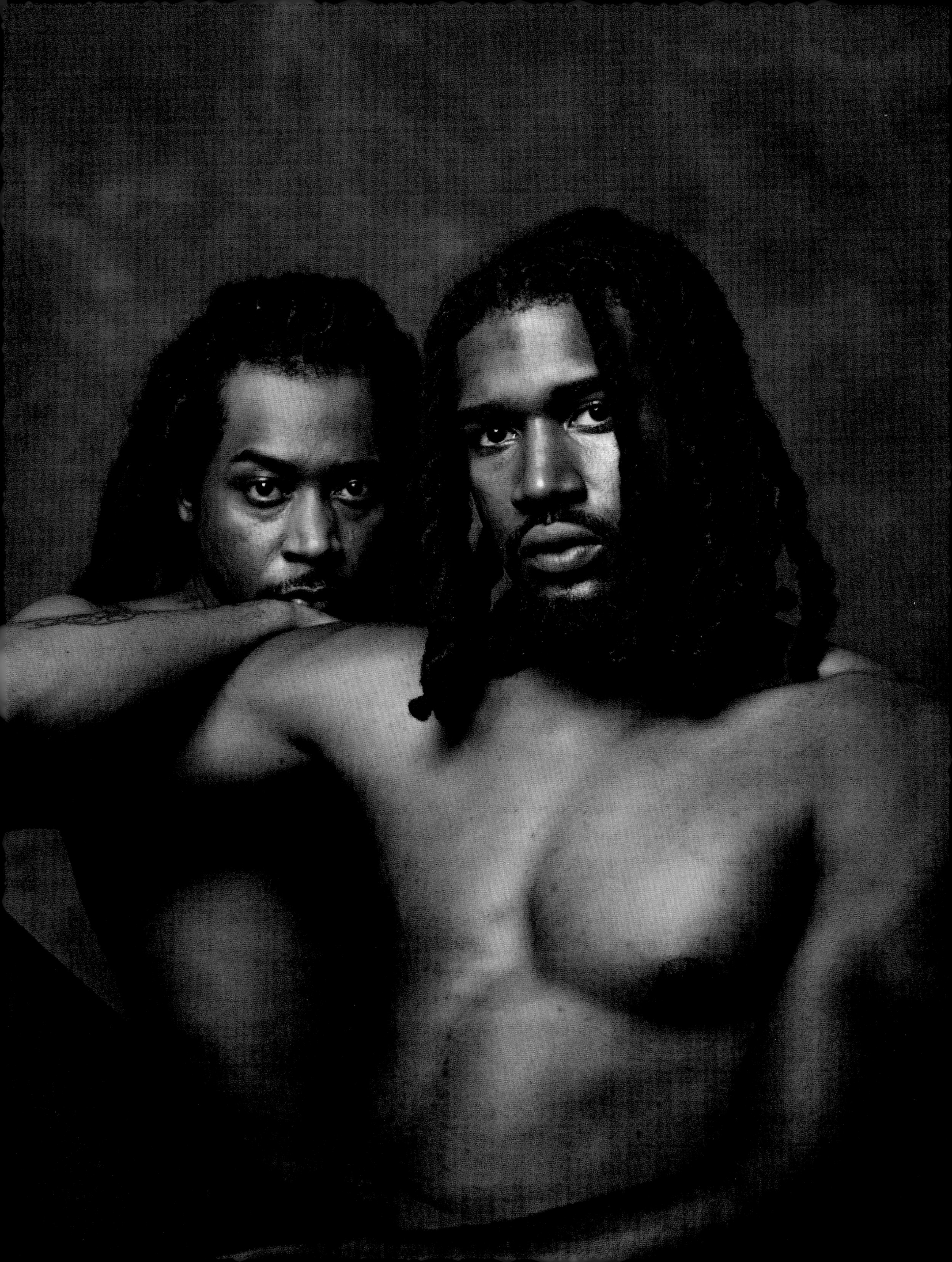

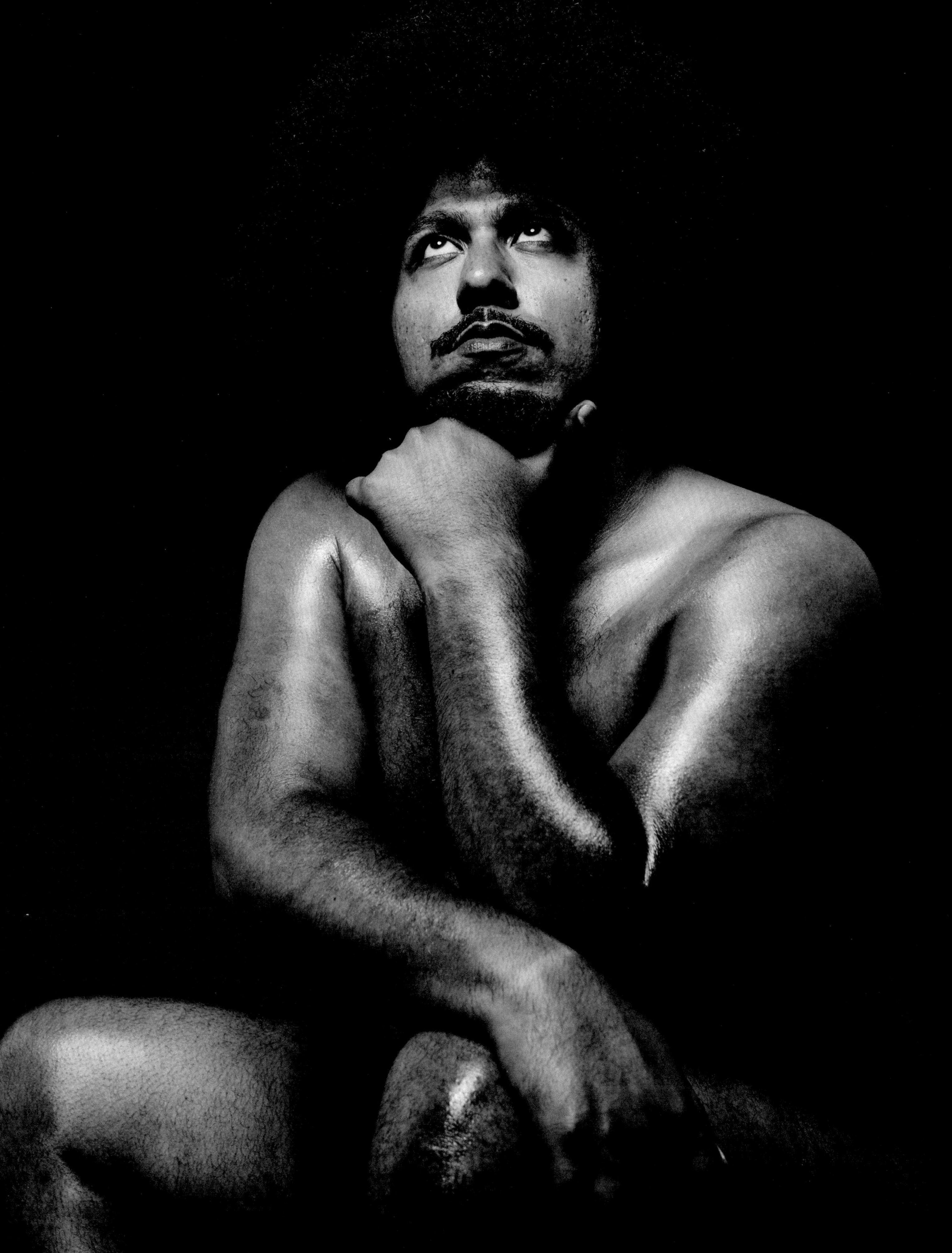

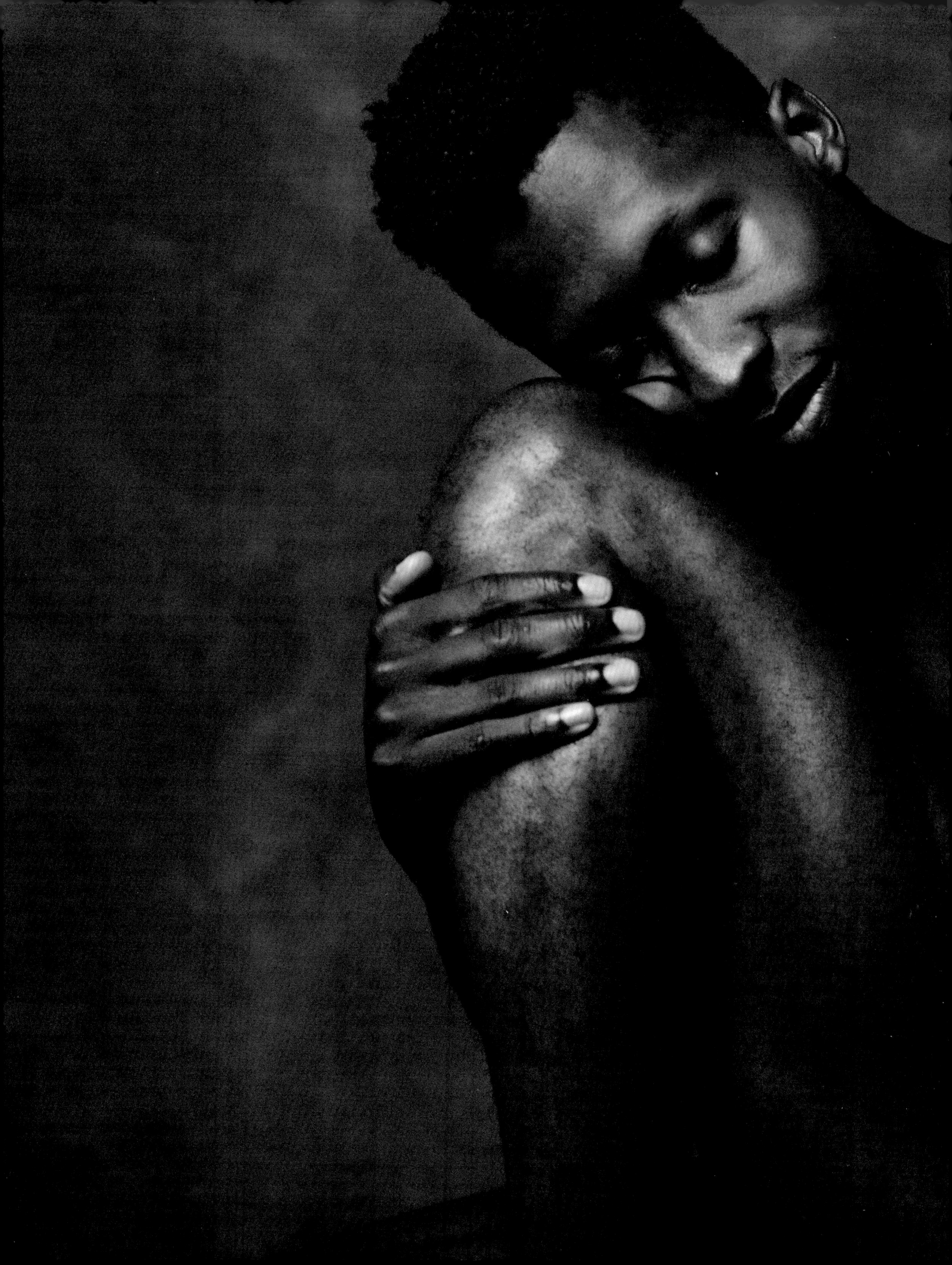

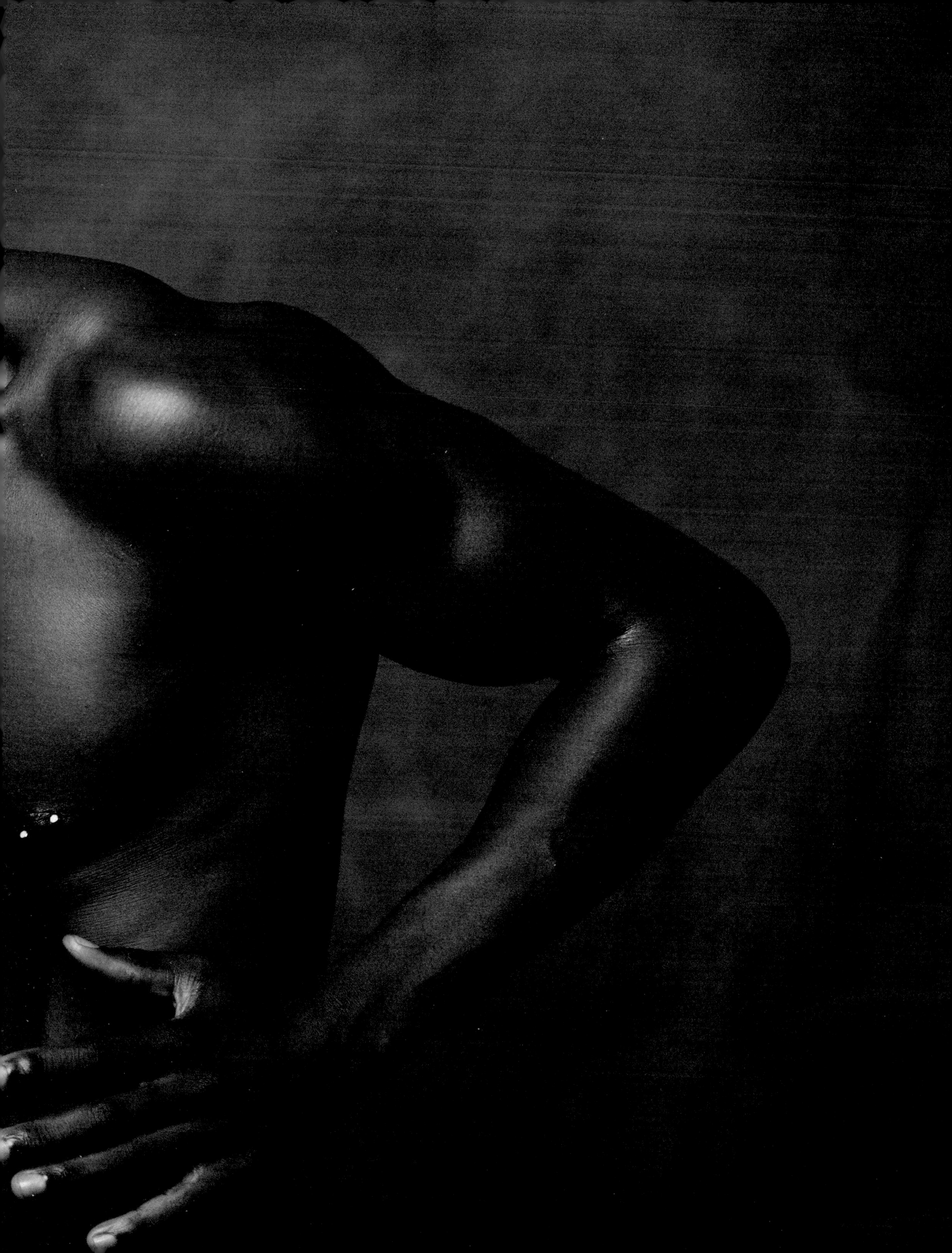

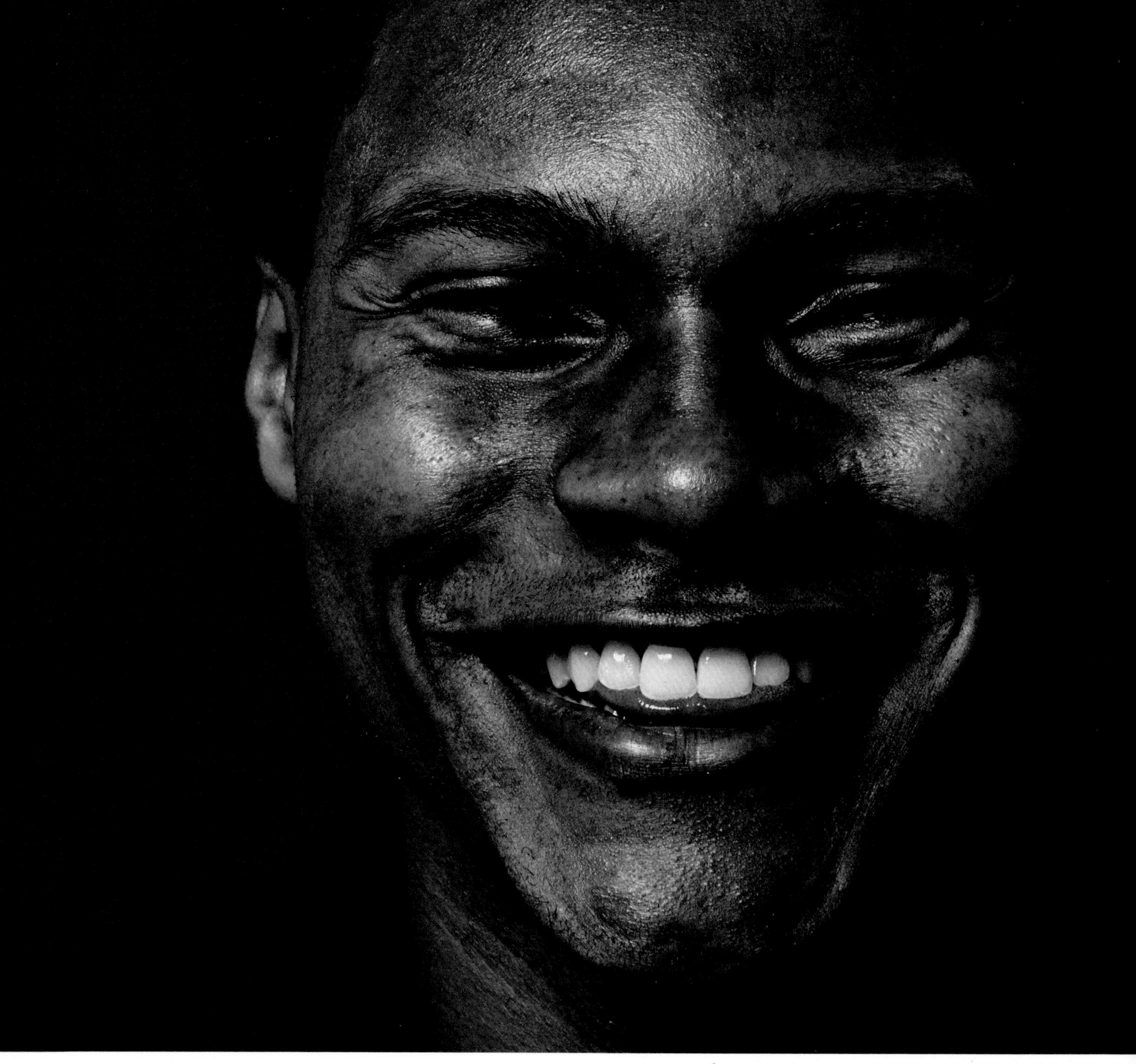

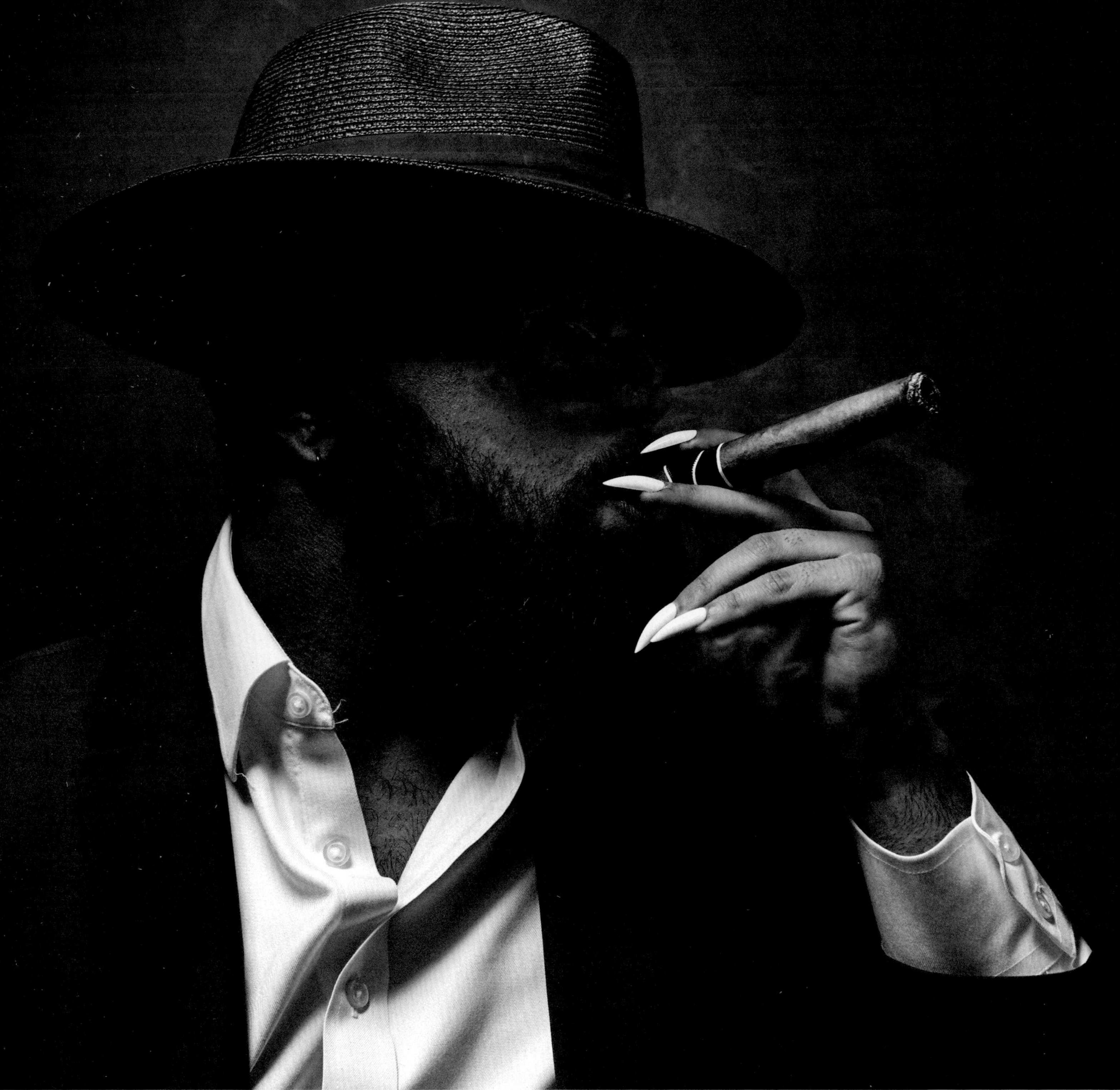

ERIC HART JR. IN CONVERSATION WITH KALEN ALLEN

Kalen Allen: Even though I had read the synopsis and was informed of what I was opening up to, what was surprising to me was that I didn't immediately think queerness, and I think the reason why that is, is because there's a perfect blend of all these elements that somewhat blur the lines. I think what the series does great is that it symbolizes, normalizing this play on the spectrum of the binary in masculinity and femininity.

Eric Hart Jr.: It really was a goal in terms of, like you said, blurring that line and creating a body of work that redefines what queerness can look like and really question what a queer photograph or a queer photo series is. I feel like a lot of photo work that I see, specifically in relation to masculinity, in relation to queerness, it's like very bright, and it's very much these certain tropes that play specifically into femininity. It was important for me to flip that so I'm happy that translated. I'm just curious if you have any favorite images? Just any of the shots that stuck out to you and why?

KA: I particularly love the photo of the three bodies in the tights with the nails because ballerinas are innately already more muscular than other people. And a lot of times female athletes are called men because of how muscular they are, you know, that was an issue that Serena Williams would run into. So when I look at these pictures, and even though men do ballet, it's the added nail part of it that kind of blurs those lines.

I have one more. The picture with the man standing naked with the white hands. Now what I thought, especially because I saw four hands, was the concept of black bodies being fetishized, specifically by white men. And we know of that senator, you know, those black boys were dying every time he was with them. So I think of stuff like that. We all know what it's like, when white men or white gay men use terms like BBC and stuff like that, you know.

EHJ: Wow, that's intriguing because I created that image with the idea of black bodies being restricted or censored, even hidden. So for it to be the opposite and be read as something that's desire is very interesting. I was trying to create a body of work that is thought-provoking and isn't always specifically on the nose in terms of what I'm trying to say about masculinity or power because I feel like it's such a broad topic. The way you define power and the way I define power can be two completely different things. And all the things that feed into that, like sexuality, religion, region, all of that. We all look at those differently. Even the title, When I Think About Power, struck me because I wanted this collection to be almost a processing of thought. The notion of thinking leads to so many conclusions. When we're thinking we draft all these potential scenarios. I wanted to create images that lend themselves to that so I am happy to hear you read that image differently.

KA: The one with the young man that has the white band-aid stripes, I was like OUU I wonder what that means.

EHJ: Specifically those images, the band-aid, that was wanting to express almost the joy and the resilience that simultaneously lives within the hardships and the trauma. Even like the nails in the images. I love me some acrylics. I keep my nails done. They're literally done right now. But I still struggle with that, like that's still a struggle for me and it's not the easiest thing to step outside with my nails done, or go visit back home with my nails done, but it makes me happy, so showing that duality of just being who you are but also still feeling that pain and that struggle. That's what the opening image is about. That's what the band-aid image is rooted in. Those images represent the notion of pride being work, which is something I think isn't discussed enough.

KA: I love that. So before starting this did you write a list of different queer themes? How did you decide on each expression of imagery?

EHJ: There was a list in terms of things that are related to power. So I didn't dive into it thinking queerness, I dove in more so thinking, what do I associate with power. So for me, religion is a big one just because I look at my grandma as very powerful, she's very religious. So things incorporated in the book like the white robes or the church hats are nods to her and my church upbringing. I feel like it takes a very powerful woman to wear that hat, so to flip that and put it on men of course lends itself well for a queer reading, but definitely started from a place of just acknowledging the power attached to this accessory. The same goes for the nail extensions. I just think that longer nails typically are associated with powerful femininity, like Catwoman, or Flo-Jo and Sha'carri Richardson. I even did some research about the nail specifically and found out that previously in the Ming dynasty and ancient Egypt women would wear nail extensions to show that they didn't have to do work. So nails were this sign of status. Or like, in Africa, nail extensions were made out of gold and ivory, so it was a sign of wealth. I was just really thinking about ways to depict power but have it take a new form.

KA: I am just interested because you're working in black and white, there's a very specific style to where it almost feels like just bodies on blackness, it's kind of like you have this inverted silhouette of people. Was there a reason to use these darker tones?

EHJ: When I thought about masculinity and queerness in terms of this contemporary photography landscape, as previously mentioned, I feel like it had a very specific look. Lots of colors. Particularly colors related to femininity. You will see black bodies laying in a bed of flowers, you will see black bodies with these colorful durags attached to them and I feel like that just wasn't for me, that just wasn't pushing the envelope enough. I respect that work and I love that work, but for me, I feel like the challenge of creating a body of work that expresses queerness, expresses masculinity but in a black and white format was almost a challenge that I wanted to take on. I found through the process of shooting black and white, using deeper shadows, as someone consuming the work you're paying more attention to the expressions and you're not lost in the color. I can really manipulate and draw your eye to what I want to draw your eye to. So I think the blackness helps in terms of the control I have with an image.

KA: I also appreciate the use of different bodies and even the use of a child. I think a lot of times that's where nobody talks about queerness, during those ages. But I remember being the kid in school and being teased and picked on all the time and I wish I would have somebody to talk to that could explain why that was or why that was happening, you know what I mean?

EHJ: Photographing children was one of those hesitancies I had with creating this series because I questioned what it means to include images of children within a queer body of work or a body of work that clearly has a queer reading. But I think when it comes to blurring what queerness is and kind of equalizing how we view queerness in this world, it was important to include that work. I feel like I've been queer my whole life, like as a kid I just felt that otherness before I could even name it. Scratching sexuality out of the conversation, I knew my interest and feelings were unique and totally opposite of my brother or my male cousins and I think including that dialogue in this work is important. One of my favorite quotes is from bell hooks and she says something to the extent of "queer not as being who you are having sex with, but queer as being about the self that is at odds with everything around it". As a kid I definitely resonated with that notion of being at odds with the world around me and I think that is what sparked this search for my own power and sense of self. Even like you just mentioned being teased as a kid, I think those experiences play so much into the struggle and challenges of internally feeling powerful and worthy. I feel like I see a lot of work confronting the outside world. The external. I think I see more work that sends messaging to the world, you know, let boys be fragile, let boys do what they want to do. But I also feel like, no one talks about the internal challenges and how what we know, what challenges do you still feel that? Or is that something you'd move on from once you grew up? Because you're someone who is so confident and just walks in their power which is why I wanted to have this conversation with you. Do you still ever have those challenges?

KA: Oh, I absolutely still experience a lot of those challenges. Just the other day I was like, a lot of who I am was built out of the lack thereof. A lot of my comedy and who I am was built out of trauma or or a need to escape or to survive. I think with that, sometimes I feel as though, well who am I really? Because I feel like so much of me is built out of pain. I think sometimes it's hard for me to let go of that pain because that's how I know how to function, and I think that's why a lot of us hold on to things that don't serve us.

It's crazy when you think about how the only people that really exist in this space are queer people. For instance, ballroom culture. We know that a large amount of that population comes from being kicked out of their homes, that's how families are built. There are all these things in life that lead you not to function like a normal human being is supposed to be able to function. You have to live with the intersectionality of blackness and being queer and having to figure out how that works in your daily life. It's practically impossible.

EHJ: That's one of the things I feel like personally, right now, I'm trying to figure out. How do I show up for myself as a black queer man on the day-to-day in ways that make me feel good? In ways that make me feel whole. In ways where I am being completely authentic to who I want to be. But also protect myself and recognize that there are times when I'm unsafe to simply be. There are times when I got to switch it up. That is just something that is always on my mind. This isn't even a question, this is just something that always is on my mind, like, how do I celebrate myself in my fullness without acknowledging and recognizing that trauma and that pain. I think ultimately this series is that grasping of the two coexisting, finding that there is power in the struggle, just as there is weakness and vulnerability within confidence. Knowing that there is power in all expressions of yourself. Let me ask you, how would you say a man who does feel more sensitive or feminine, how does he put power back into that? When society is telling you this thing strips you of your power, how do you specifically as a black queer man use femininity as power?

KA: It really lies in the authenticity of being unapologetic about who you are. Your existence alone is revolutionary so just existing is enough sometimes. Existing in a way that is not modified, that is no code-switching, that is not assimilating. That is just saying, I don't live on any spectrum of this. I'm

To every powerful soul I got the privilege of photographing for the series, I thank you for your
time and presence. Thank you for believing in this vision and lending yourself to these frames.
I give the utmost love and appreciation to the Damiani family. Silvia Pesci, Eleonora Pasqui and
Lorenzo Tugnoli, this wouldn't be possible without the work you put in. Fred Sands IV, you are a
master of your craft and I thank you for all your artistic input and direction. You all played such
pivotal roles in making this book happen and for that, I am forever grateful.

I thank the contributors for not only being a part of this project but for offering complexities and
truth in their dialogue. The three of you inspire me in ways you can't even imagine. Kalen, thank
you for being you, always. The pride and authenticity you give to yourself are contagious.
Wholeheartedly, I walk with my head a little higher because of you. Chi, your brilliance and
desire to bring good to this world shines in all that you do. Thank you for the work you are doing.
Lastly, Zun, I am so grateful this series has brought you into my life as a friend and mentor.
I thank you for challenging me and playing therapist in moments when I questioned my own
power. Every single conversation we had I not only walked away inspired creatively but mentally
empowered to be a man of truth.

Dr. Deborah Willis, you are a light not only in my life but for so many others as well, and I thank
you for sharing your spirit, kindness, and love for the craft of image-making with this world. I am
galvanized by your wisdom, and I thank you from the bottom of my heart for your mentorship.

To my beautiful family and friends, Grandma Vickie, Aunt Tina, Daddy, Junior, Zay, Aunt Pat and
the crew, RJ, Lauryn, Timya, and Jada. I thank you for constantly loving and supporting me
even in times when you didn't know how. I find power in who I am through an amalgamation of
your voices and hope all of you know how much I love you. None of this would have
been possible without this village you all have built around me.

I give thanks to every artist, creative, and friend who took the time to offer critique, feedback,
and guidance during this process such as Elijah Heyward III, Isolde Brielmaier, Eric Johnson, Lorie
Novak, Bayeté Ross Smith, Tyler Mitchell, Trey Dickenson, Jaé Joseph, Antoine Grégory, Elliott
Jerome Brown Jr., Kendall Bessent, Antoine Manning, Danny Dunson, Joshua Renfroe,
Sean Howard, Evan Reeves, Brandon Fousheé, Zak Krevitt and Rhia Hylton.

Lastly, I just give thanks to all the Black queer creative voices that inspire me to walk in my truth
and stand in my power.

Love you all. Thank you.

WHEN I
THINK
ABOUT
POWER